CW00376356

The Man In The Sun Sent Me To Hell

The Man In The Sun Sent Me To Hell

"Dear Debbie"

Enjoy Try this Book
Dar Cay + "lovely you"

X

JANETTE MILLS

Janette Mills

X

© Janette Mills, 2013

Published by Bainbridge Press

All rights reserved. No part of this book may be reproduced, adapted, stored in a retrieval system or transmitted by any means, electronic, mechanical, photocopying, or otherwise without the prior written permission of the author.

The rights of Janette Mills to be identified as the author of this work have been asserted in accordance with the Copyright, Designs and Patents Act 1988.

Disclaimer
This story is based on true events of the author's experiences, although names have been changed for privacy reasons.

A CIP catalogue record for this book is available from the British Library.

ISBN 978-0-9927086-0-3

Prepared and printed in the UK

Introduction

U pon thinking what to write, I reflected on the fact that one of my oldest friend's first husband died this year. It gave me the incentive to really want to write about my many experiences. I have always been totally open with people about my life, and I was saddened to realise how much hurt we inflict by keeping things from people. My friend had always longed to know who her Father was, but her Mother died last year, keeping this secret, and so she will never know. Also one of my cousins only found out last year that she had a sister, her Mother also died, keeping this secret. They were war babies. She traced this sister, only to find that she died aged fifty-six, but had two daughters.

So from here I will begin on my writing journey. It involves love, passion, violence, excitement, four wonderful children and eleven amazing grandchildren; but I never let my hell get the better of me. My greatest sorrow is not to have been the thespian I could have been, with my opera and acting. This is the summary of the beginning of my story.

Chapter One

I want to start the story of my sixty-plus year journey at the end and work my way back, as we all know it's easier to search your mind backwards. In my life I have had to take time to keep afloat on this ever-rocky boat. I've nearly drowned so many times with heartbreak, solitude and endless love which has pained my children, grandchildren, friends and my fellow man until it has broken me and taken the sight from my right eye. Only now this has made me see more clearly and take pen to paper, to fulfil a dream hopefully – a dream of giving people hope however hopeless things may seem. I am your ambassador for attitude to life; with strength you will get there.

This is 2012 – a bad year for me health-wise – three strokes; but what brought me to this? I will begin.

In early 2011 I went to Spain, once again, to visit my friend Connie. I was so excited as I loved the town. She lived in the sunshine with many great friendships, and just around the corner was the beautiful Albia, then the Altea Hills and the wonderful coast; so you can see why I loved it there. I was picked up by Connie at the bus-station adjacent to Alicante airport in the early evening; it was lovely and warm on the drive to Alfaz. Connie suggested we stop and have a drink in a nice wine bar just outside the town. The laughter began from our first glass of wine, then we were on our way again.

We parked in the town's car park with my cases still in the back seat. Connie said, "Let's go to *Robin's Nest* to see Earma and Robin!" As this was the start of my holiday I could not agree more. The place was buzzing; Earma and Robin were pleased to see me and we were having so much fun. A Spanish local who owned a plant-nursery asked Connie if he could buy me to have as his own! He only spoke Spanish, so Connie relayed this to me. Everyone was so happy. There was a bar-stool behind me – the only empty seat in the pub. It had remained empty until about 11.30 p.m. when I turned to find a man now sitting on it. "Hello" he said. He was English, very tall and had grey hair. I replied of course, turned back to my company, and then was drawn to turn around again by his question, "Would you like a drink?"

"I am with my friend." I replied

"Well she can have one too?" So we accepted. This man and I started up a conversation, he began with "Could you love me?" Well I was just so surprised by his straight question that I replied with, "You never know." It was like déjà vu from something that had happened in 1988. We didn't stop talking and laughing from there on in.

After Earma and Robin shut the bar they came with us all to the Spanish bar up in the square. By 2 a.m. I was sitting on his knee and we kissed! I had never kissed like that before in my thirty-plus years of marriage. He was separated and had been slowly drinking himself into his grave for the past ten months. At 3 a.m. we all parted; Phil (that was his name) took a taxi to Polop, but not before giving me his home telephone number on a sticky piece of green paper. To this very day I still have that little piece of paper, stuck in the same place in the back of my address book. He said to me, "Please call me tomorrow. I want you to come to my villa. I have never felt so happy." With a parting kiss he sped off in the taxi. We got one of my cases out of Connie's car and walked down the hill feeling tired, tiddly, warm and happy.

The next day Connie stayed in bed a little later than usual, but this did not make a difference to my usual early rising. I had this excitement in the pit of my stomach, the desire to see this man again. It was around 12 p.m. when I decided to ring him. Connie was now up and we had just gone for a walk with the little darling Frankie – a fabulous corgi who was almost human, but not quite, thank goodness! I was almost ready to faint when I rang; he answered quite quickly saying, "I was so hoping you would call, are you coming?"

"Yes, Connie is bringing me. Could she stay too?"

"Of course, I can't wait until you get here!"

"It will be around 2 p.m. if that's okay?"

Connie and I had a light lunch then got ourselves ready. I put on a pretty, blue dress but felt like I could hardly breathe with the anticipation of meeting this man again. All the bad seemed to become good. Connie put on her bikini and a sundress; Phil had said there was a pool and we would be welcome to swim, so I packed my swimsuit. We were a little late as we took a wrong turning into Polop, which is about ten kilometres from Alfaz. He was waiting at the gate when we arrived, and how lovely it was to see him again in the light of day. He told me that I looked beautiful and I said that he was very handsome. We had a drink then he gently kissed me and asked if I would walk up to the church at the other side of town; he warned that it was very steep but said that he had always wanted to do it. Well I was just like a helpless puppy, "I would love to" I said. Connie declined and asked if she could stay by the pool and just read her book. Phil told her of course she could as he wasn't expecting anybody.

What a wonderful walk we had – chatting, holding hands and looking at the lovely scenery. Phil was so pleased I had gone with him as he had longed to do it, along with many other things, for over ten years but no-one would ever go with him. He took some photographs of me and then some kind people took some of us both together. We walked back down to the bottom of the hill where we stopped to gaze at each other and share a kiss. I felt safe with his tenderness and he kept twiddling the little ring on my finger. He suddenly stopped and shouted, "Oh fuck! There's my wife in my car, bitch!"

"Does it matter?"

"No, she is just so vindictive. Never mind, don't let it spoil our lovely day." He gently squeezed my hand and kissed my lips. I had a feeling that this was going to be the start of the hell, but I put it to the back of my mind.

We carried on around the corner to a little Spanish bar as we were so thirsty. Everyone seemed to know Phil, and they made a fuss of me, saying they hadn't seen him so happy for a long time. It was a good feeling! We left feeling very happy; he gently kissed me again saying, "I wanted to see if last night was real. I have never felt kisses like yours before, my whole being lights up!"

When we returned to the villa Connie was still reading by the pool, she told us, "I was just dozing earlier and a man appeared. He asked who I was and I asked the same. He said he was your brother Phil, so I told him you had gone for a walk with my friend Janette." By this time it was about 7 p.m. and we were all starving. Phil put the BBQ on for the meat and Connie and I made some food – Connie her special coleslaw and I a nice starter and some vegetables. Phil had wanted to use his BBQ for a long time but had always been jeered about it; well what a success it was! It was such a wonderful evening – food, wine, warmth, swimming, a nice man; what else could anyone ask for? Connie left at 9.30 p.m. as she had to be up for work the next day; Phil said he would see me home in a taxi. His brother Damian appeared later and we had a lovely time around the bar. Damian's wife Martha joined us; well how jealousy does at first show itself as a friend. How was I to know how she would truly turn out to be? She was unkempt, very round and unfortunately fancied Phil. I went along with the laughter; I had yet to learn a lot about them from Phil. It would not shock me however; I think that by now I am incapable of shock, especially after my third very violent marriage. But what I also did not know is that Phil was very easily swayed and cajoled. Weak would be the best word to describe him.

It was quite late when they left. At last alone, we sat and had a quiet drink whilst talking and sharing endless kisses. I left for Connie's around 2 a.m. in a taxi, feeling that at last I had got my bit of heaven. I never thought that it would be the hell that nearly ended my life.

Chapter Two

The next day I went to work with Connie; we went on a trip to Alicante. I just loved seeing what this town was all about. There was the coast, a big marina, cruise liners and yachts coming in from all parts of the ocean; most people fly into Alicante and think that the airport is all that's there. We spent our lunchtime sitting by the marina, "Oh I just love being here!" I said to Connie. We sat talking mostly about Phil and how I couldn't wait to see him again. A voice said, "Is that Janette?" and on the next table sat three guys. I couldn't believe it, they had sailed all the way from the boat club in York where I used to franchise, what a small world! We shared a few laughs but then we had to move on as we only had a limited amount of time before we had to be back at the coach. How happy I felt; I had a warm feeling as I was seeing Phil again that evening. We travelled back to Albia, overjoyed that we'd had such a lovely day.

Connie had to go to work the next day so she didn't join me in going out for the evening. She was very welcome to join Phil and me but she declined. I met Phil at *Robin's Nest*, how lovely it was to see him again. He smothered me in his arms and gave me kisses repeatedly. We ordered drinks, then after a short while he asked if I would mind him going over the road, as his youngest son was in the bar opposite. I said I was quite happy for him to do so as I knew most of the people in *Robin's Nest*. A short time passed and I looked up to see Phil coming into the bar with a tall, dark-haired young man. Phil introduced his youngest son as Kyle, who promptly leaned over to give me a hug and a kiss. He gave me no indication of what the next son and his Mother would bring. He stayed for a while then said his goodbyes. When he was gone Phil and I spent a lovely night chatting before going for something to eat. He ordered a taxi and we shared a million kisses; when he dropped me off he shouted, "Get some things and stay with me!" as we were going to the safari park the next day. I did as I was asked and the happiness was oozing from our pores. The night was a night of soft music, holding and loving each other. I never thought that I would feel the way I did. We slept in each other's arms and I can't remember ever having felt so safe.

The next morning, Phil had to leave me to go and collect his car from his estranged wife. He sped off on his motorbike but I did not feel afraid, quite the opposite! I had a swim and then got ready. It seemed an age that Phil was gone, but this all became clear when he arrived back with the car, "I have had such a hard time getting my car for one day. She wanted to know if it was so I could take out the blonde she saw me with the other day. She didn't want you going in it, and I had to put up with her for half an hour! But I got it in the end."

We set off to the safari park; it was very large and we were there a long time. We got to the reptile house and Phil had forgotten his glasses so I read everything aloud to him as I could read without glasses. He was so amazed by my tender reading; we gained some followers and I felt like the reptile house guide! I did not know then that my darling would turn into a reptile himself, but I should have learnt by then after my many life experiences. I wasn't being careful though as this was just for me, not for my children, but for me alone.

The next day was just as wonderful as the last. We went for a walk in the warm sun; holding hands I felt so happy. Phil looked at me and asked, "Are you feeling the same as me? Totally happy?"

"Yes, yes!" was my answer. We just stood and kissed and it was like drifting into another being. I thought, "Please God don't let this end!" When we came back down to Earth we did some shopping then went back to Phil's villa. I cooked for us and we ate with such delight, feeding each other. I felt wonderful as I love having someone to share my happiness with.

The next day we went into Alfaz. We spent the whole morning, until lunchtime, just talking. I found it so exhilarating – everything I was feeling and finding out so much about each other. After lunch I caught up with Connie and her friend Jane. We went off into Benidorm to have a few hours on the beach; Phil did not do beaches so he went off to run some errands. We went back at tea-time and met Phil at *Robin's Nest*. He took us all for a nice meal then back to his villa. We returned to Connie's later in the evening as we were spending the next day together. "Goodnight darling" he whispered, "I have fallen in love with you. I am waiting for our next meeting." He kissed me with such gentle passion that we felt like one.

Chapter Three

The next day Connie and I went into beautiful Albia, where we walked along the front in the warm, gentle wind. I couldn't help letting my thoughts drift to Phil but I tried not to talk about him. We walked up to Altea harbour where I treated Connie to a meal for her friendship and kindness. After this we made our way back home to get ready to spend the evening in Benidorm. All of the girls went and some of the men, but Phil did not come as he felt sad and low; this is when I should have seen the signs. We had a great night laughing, drinking and dancing until the early hours. Royston, one of the bar owners from Alfaz, was a fabulous dancer and he danced with me a lot as I was the best out of the girls. Phil called me at around 4 a.m. saying he couldn't sleep and that he was silly not to have come to Benidorm. I declined his offer to go to him, as Connie and I had already planned our Sunday together.

On Sunday morning Connie and I did a few chores, took Frankie for a walk and then went to Royston's place for Sunday lunch. It was very nice. Later on Connie, Jane, Royston and I went to Benidorm again but Phil was still sad and moping; when would he snap out of it? He was missing out on so many precious times.

On Monday 18th April Connie had planned a trip for us on her coach tours. We were all waiting with apprehension to see whether or not Phil would turn up. He was coming to Alfaz on his motorbike and we were all driving to Albir in Connie's car. Her boyfriend had stayed overnight so we were all at the front of the house, waiting. He arrived at the last minute; I was so pleased to see him, although he looked ragged around the edges. He had obviously been drinking heavily and I felt sad. He shook hands with Connie's boyfriend Sam who said, "Hello Phil, I'm a smuggler." Sam went off and we got on our way.

On the coach, Phil and I burst into laughter about the way that Sam had introduced himself. Phil said, "He just came out with 'I'm a smuggler!' I could have been a detective for all he knew!" It was a wonderful journey; we went to Costa Blanca, Calpe and Avià. The caves were fantastic and we had some great photographs taken. Still reeling from such a fantastic day, we went to a fish restaurant in Murcia. The food and service were both excellent. We sat in the sun, holding hands and looking into each other's eyes. Phil said that if he could never see my eyes again then he would not want to go on living. That was one of the things he said to me when we had our first kiss. He leaned over, still kissing me and said, "You gave me my life back. You saved me. I will always be yours." That evening I went back to Phil's and stayed over; tenderness and loving is all I remember.

The next day we went to Albia for a lovely walk. We stopped for tapas and drinks; I was drowning in happiness.

In the evening, I reluctantly packed my things as I had to fly back home. Phil didn't want me to leave but I could not stay.

Connie drove me to a lovely restaurant so that I could meet Phil. I sat and waited for him; when he arrived he looked wonderful. He said that I was the most beautiful woman he had ever known and he did not want to be without me. We ate at *Anthea Park*, sitting on the balcony, watching the world go by. I felt that I had it all right there. We sang for the owners and they loved it, but it all ended so quickly and soon it was time to go. I spent the night laying in Phil's arms.

I left his villa at 7 a.m. the next morning and he was very upset. He asked me over and over not to go, but I had to catch my flight and Connie was driving me to the airport. "I will see you soon, I love you!" were his parting words,

"And I love you!" We kissed, then I was gone. The tears were flowing down my face; I did not want to leave this man! Shaking, I got on my flight and I never stopped thinking about him the whole way home.

Chapter Four

I arrived home early and had two of my darling grandchildren to stay overnight. We went out walking the next day and had a lovely time at the skate-park. When we got back I made something nice to eat and my little sweetheart Jill asked, "Have you got a millionaire boyfriend Nana?"

"I feel like a millionaire myself with all this love from you! But my man-friend is just a nice man and we have felt like millionaires since meeting each other." The time came for them to leave and I missed them so much when they had gone. I was sat reflecting on things when the phone rang; it was a voice I adored – Phil! "I cannot bear being here without you so I have booked a flight to Leeds Bradford airport. I will be with you early in the morning."

"I can't believe it," I screeched, "I won't sleep, I am so happy!" We were just like teenagers.

The next morning, I busied myself whilst waiting for him to come. My stomach was doing tipple-tails. It was now 10 a.m. and he was an hour late. I was worried that something had happened. Another hour passed – it was endless! Then all of a sudden the panic stopped, as I looked out of the window to see a man getting out of a cab. My heart was beating at 100 miles an hour. I opened the front door and we fell into each other's arms. "I have missed you so," he said, "you look so wonderful. Your eyes are something I cannot bear the thought of not seeing again." We kissed until we thought we might stop breathing; how happy we were.

After our lips parted we began to talk with breathless excitement. You would have thought that we had been separated for months! We gradually settled down so I made coffee whilst Phil took his bag upstairs. I wondered whether this was really happening – was the man I had fallen for in Spain now here in my home in England? It felt so right. My heart was full and I had the partner I had always wanted.

It was a nice day, so I decided to take Phil on a delightful walk along the river and into town. He had never been to York before so I was excited about showing him everything and showing off my man! We went to a favourite pub of mine and he loved the whole ambience of it. I showed him round the town and he was getting a good feeling about it, "I love this town," he said, "It makes me feel like I want to live in England, especially with you here my gorgeous woman! I love you so much." We went home on the bus; he was so giddy! At home we had a rest and just held each other like we were one.

That evening we went out for a drink and to my favourite Indian restaurant. Phil loved the food; I had been going there for years, and he agreed that it was the best. The half-hour walk home turned into two hours as we kept stopping and kissing. He held my face in his hands and said, "I want to look at your face, see your eyes, and feel your lips. Is this my heaven? It must be." By the time we got home it was late, so we just went to bed and fell into each other's arms. We happily fell asleep on each other's lips.

The next few days went along nicely; Phil loved everything we did. I took him on the bar-walls then we visited the Minster. We climbed the two-hundred-and-forty steps to the top; the only problem was that Phil had eaten at York's famous fish and chip shop so he was a very uncomfortable man the whole day.

The next four days were wonderful – full of fun! Phil loved being in York and said, "I could live here with you with this ecstatic love I feel, and in a lovely city; what more could a man want?" I had given this man his life back and provided him with a purpose to go on. "I never want this to end." He would whisper every night, kissing my lips. "You are the man meant for me."

"And you are the woman I have fallen helplessly in love with. I have never known such a love." Was this my heaven at last?

On Easter Monday we sat around in the morning and went for a walk a little bit later on. We walked by my sister's hotel as it was just a stone's throw away from my house. They were out in the garden so I introduced Phil to my sister and niece. "You're just what my sister has been looking for – someone to love, have fun and travel with." She told him. Phil leaned over and kissed me. I just felt ecstatic. We said our goodbyes and got on our way to my Son's house for a meal. My son and daughter-in-law had a bed-and-breakfast a few doors down from my sister's hotel. Phil was made very welcome but he felt uncomfortable for the first time since arriving in York; I did not yet know why, as his real nature was still hidden deep inside and his vicious jealousy was yet to be shown.

We left in the early evening as we went for a nice walk. I took Phil to a quaint pub in an area just by my house – the quiz was taking place and we both thoroughly enjoyed taking part. After an enjoyable night we walked home once more, Phil told me that he felt he had wasted his life living without our beautiful love. We had a night cap then went to bed, so loved up. Phil laid on me funny and I felt a soaring pain in my side – I knew he had cracked my rib but I didn't complain, I just gritted my teeth. I did so for the next six weeks – Phil was having such a bad time that I didn't want him to feel any more shit; he'd had enough of that and so had I.

Chapter Five

The next day we went to town along by the river. On the way back we called in at *Plonker's* for some refreshments and food, then we were on our way home again. I was so happy, apart from the surging pain in my side, but I did not complain. At home, Phil sat outside while I made some tea. My youngest son came round and seemed to get along very well with Phil. I made us a nice lamb dinner with all the trimmings. My son helped to clear the table and then left as he had an early start for work the next morning.

The next day I found myself reluctantly giving in to Phil and getting on a train to go and see his family in Market Rasen. He had been pestering me for days about going to meet his Mum but I'd told him it was too soon, "Mum will love you," he promised, "I want to show you off to my family." So we were on our way. We arrived in Market Rasen and Phil said, "I had forgotten what a one-armed town this is. But let me just get my bearings and we will find the place where we are meeting my brother. He is going to give us a lift to Mum's in Owersby." We ended up in a small watering-hole and Phil ordered us a small lager while we waited. We were both ready for a drink as we had made three changes whilst on the train journey. Of course I was very nervous about meeting his family. After a short while a man appeared. I knew he was Phil's brother straight away – he was younger, very smart and attractive. We got on immediately so it was easy; he had a drink then we were on our way to Phil's Mum's house. I didn't know what to expect!

Graham (Phil's brother's name) said a quick hello to his Mum and then left. I was greeted with such kindness; she was so impressed with me and was of course pleased to see her son looking so happy. She offered us a drink and Phil said that he would stick to coffee as we would be going out later – this I was very pleased about. She was a very clean lady with a very clean house; she was badly bent over as she had broken her back when she'd fallen onto a piano some years ago. She had six sons, of which one was deceased, and her husband had also been deceased for many years. All of a sudden the door opened and in walked Matt, another of Phil's brothers. He was a couple of years older than Phil and more portly, but with the same look. He was very funny and we got on right away. Phil and his brother chatted away and I felt so pleased that they had taken to me, "but then again," I thought, "Why shouldn't they?" After all, I had given Phil his life back. Listening to their chat, I had an uneasy feeling, but I dismissed it as I didn't want to end the feeling I had that I was whole again.

The next day we took a trip into Market Rasen; there wasn't a lot to do, but we had a walk around and a few drinks in the square. Matt came and took us back to Phil's

Mum's as we were all going out that night for a curry. Graham and Tina came too and Matt took us all, but he decided not to join us himself. The meal was average but afterwards we went to a nightclub and had a lovely time dancing and drinking. True to his word, Matt came back for us at 2 a.m. and took us to Phil's Mum's where we immediately fell asleep.

On Saturday Phil's Aunty and Uncle came round with their son and daughter-in-law. It was like a café in the kitchen as I spent my time making food for everyone; as cooking is one of my loves, I didn't mind and just got stuck in. They all thought that I was wonderful and Phil's Aunty May said that she had never seen anyone as pretty as me.

During the afternoon Graham and Phil went to play golf; everyone else left so I decided to cook lunch for them all on Sunday. Matt took us to the supermarket so that we could buy everything for the 10 guests we would have. I made a super meal and everyone was over the moon; Phil's Mum Vera kept saying that she couldn't believe I had made Yorkshire puddings too! I had also made cake and a crumble. Everyone cleared up together and it was thoroughly enjoyable. Vera said that she had never known so much loving, which was nice of her.

The evening was just as great – we went to see a band at an unusual venue in Market Rasen. Graham and Tina came with us, along with their daughter Helen and some friends. Phil and I were so loved up; everyone said it was good to see us so happy. I felt so safe and warm as he kept kissing me and saying, "I love you, I am so happy with you. I want to feel like this forever, it's something I've never felt before."

The next day Phil, Graham and I went golfing; it was a very windy course at Rasen. Afterwards we went for a drink, then Graham dropped us back at Phil's Mum's. We told Vera that we'd had a nice time, then suddenly Phil just blew up! Apparently, the day I arrived Graham had called Matt and told him to get round to Vera's house because Phil had brought a real tasty bird home. He shouted at me, asking if I fancied his brother because I'd said that a piece of clothing would suit him and he also asked if I thought that Graham was better looking than him, "Of course not," I said, "Phil you are the beauty in my eyes!" But he wouldn't let it go. He ended up walking out of the house yelling, "Why don't you go an fuck my brother?" I ran after him and caught hold of his hand; he ripped it away, taking part of my thumb nail with it. There was a soaring pain up my hand and it was bleeding everywhere; it was such a silly way for him to behave. I went back indoors and was very upset, but I decided not to accept this behaviour from him. I took myself to Phil's brother's house and his wife let me in saying, "He's in the lounge with Matt." I questioned whether, once again, I was dealing with a jealous child. As soon as he saw me, Phil started to laugh, "You won't put up with my bad behaviour will you?"

"No I won't!" came my reply. So he asked me to sit on his knee and he hugged me. "Right, I'm going back to your Mum's to start cooking tea."

Matt came round later on to take us into the country for a drink; the places we went to were nice but very deserted. In the last place we finished, Matt and I sat talking whilst Phil spent the rest of the evening stood at the bar, talking to the landlady who was a rough lesbian. But Phil could just talk away to anyone.

When we arrived back at his Mum's, she shared a night cap with us then went to bed at about midnight. We ventured up to bed at around 2 a.m. and our love making was so wonderful. Phil left all his demons behind him. We were in the last strokes of our love making when the door opened and a figure stood there, asking if she should shut the little window for us. I couldn't believe it, this woman had said her saving grace was that she had no trouble getting to sleep and staying that way. We hadn't been noisy, so I thought it very strange. Phil just said, "Fucking hell!" and I laughed and sarcastically said, "Come in why don't you? Join us?" She was gone in a flash! I couldn't understand what her reason was for disturbing us, we had been as quiet as two church mice.

The next day was moving day – to the five star hotel in Market Rasen. I loved this. His Mum told everyone about what had happened the night before and how I'd told her to join us; for God's sake, did she not realise it was a joke?

Chapter Six

We spent the day in Lincoln city; it was so nice. We had such a giggle about the night before. Phil bought some clothes and was pleased as he didn't have things with him that suited the English climate. We ate in the city in the early evening and then caught the train back to our hotel in Market Rasen. We showered and changed, then went out for a drink in the square. Phil sat on a bar stool and I stood between his legs while he kissed me and gazed into my eyes. He said, "There are a hundred people who wish they were in my place right now, but you're all mine." I had heard this before and it frightened me.

Phil was very restless back at the hotel. Our big room had a lovely veranda, and he went outside for a smoke. I followed him and asked, "What is wrong my darling?"

"I love you so much but I'm not treating you as I should. I don't want to leave you to go back to the rig, but I must so I can earn money." He was a tortured soul who had spent the past four years going backwards and forwards between the rig and the villa where he was treated like a stranger and had no intimacy. He was afraid to leave his life in Spain as he had encouraged his wife to move there to try to salvage their marriage, after he had caught her having an affair with his best friend. She constantly reminded him that he had taken her away from her home and her family and left her with nothing. Their two sons had come to live with them and Phil got them all into a lot of trouble with money. He developed a drinking problem and was never sober. Out on the veranda he opened up to me about this, releasing his ghosts, but then he said, "This is enough. Tomorrow I will tell all. The sun's going to shine and we will stay here another night." At last we crawled into bed and in each other's arms found sleep.

The next morning, as predicted by Phil, it was sunny. We had a lovely breakfast at the hotel and afterwards we went for a lovely walk. We had coffee, bought some bottles of red wine and went back to our lovely room. The veranda was a beautiful place to be in the sun; we had our wine and stayed out there all afternoon. We shared many laughs and Phil took lots of photographs of us. We felt so happy just to be with each other. All too soon it was time to get ready for our evening meal and Phil had invited his Mother to dine with us. He went out to get some cigarettes and I had a shower. He arrived back with his Mum, so I sat her out on the veranda with a cup of tea whilst we quickly got ready. The food was disappointing and Vera wasn't happy with anything. We got her a taxi home then Phil and I had a night cap. Phil had a very restless night – his demons were bothering him again. I wished that we could both just float away.

The next day it was back to Phil's Mum's. Phil was very quiet all day and decided to just paint his Mum's fence for her. In the evening we went out with his brother, which was very pleasant. We knew that it was to be our last night together for some time so we nearly squeezed the life out of each other.

It was time to leave and Phil had to go back to Spain as he had lots to sort out; he did not want to go and he didn't want me to leave him. I didn't want to go either. Our parting at Market Rasen train station was so emotional; on the platform was a very young man who was also travelling to York, so Phil asked if he would look after me. We became good friends, Josh and I. Our chattering amongst Phil's phone calls made the time pass more easily, as leaving Phil was heart wrenching.

On Saturday Phil was flying back to Spain. He was not happy, but we said our goodbyes on the phone, "Don't let it be too long darling," he said, "I will be in touch as soon as I am home. Your unbelievable love has given me my life back, I can't say it enough. Kisses!" I was missing him already, but I came home to my wonderful grandchildren Jack and Jill. They came to sleep over and we went to the local pub for tea. We had a very giggly time; I felt about seventeen! I hadn't spoken to Phil since Saturday morning so I was worried about him, knowing that he got so low so quickly. Still, I had lots of people round for Sunday lunch to take my mind off it.

The next few days I happily spent doing various things with family and friends. Phil rang me, asking me to go back to Spain so I booked my flight for 19th May. He wanted me to stay with him at the villa, but I told him that I'd spend a few days at my friend Connie's. I knew that he had been apart from his wife for a long time, but

I did not like to be in another woman's home. Still, I said I would think about it.

The next five days were good as I kept myself busy going to the races with my sons, going to see my grandson perform in his gymnastics show, having people round and speaking to Phil. He was so pleased I was going back, he told me, "I can't wait to look into those wonderful eyes and kiss your lips."

I hadn't heard from Phil for two days and was becoming worried. My grandson came to stay on the 18th and as he had just learnt to drive, he was taking me to the airport the next morning. In the evening I popped round to my friend's house and Phil called while I was out. He told my grandson that he had a bad problem but he would still be there to pick me up in Alicante. I called him back when I returned home and he told me that he'd been locked up for two days. He said he'd explain all when he saw me.

I had a really good flight with a lovely gang of girls from Huddersfield; we parted at the airport but exchanged numbers. I caught the bus to Benidorm and when I arrived at the bus station I saw Phil waiting with a taxi, just like he'd said. I jumped up and shouted, "There's my man!" He saw me off the bus and then we fell into each other. "Let's get in the cab and I'll explain everything when we get to my place in Polop." He said. I felt happy, but concerned at the same time. We arrived at Phil's home and I was too happy to be worried about anything. Phil carried my things in then held me saying, "I love you, I love you. I just want to love you for the rest of the day. I will tell you the nasty details later, I am too happy at the moment." I thought this seemed like a nice idea. It started to gently rain; warm rain, warm hearts.

In the early evening we walked up the hill to the next village. We had a very large umbrella and were singing in the rain, of course! At the top of the hill was a lovely restaurant looking over Polop. The view was spectacular. We ate and Phil told me what had led to him being locked up – His wife had gone to the villa as Phil wanted the keys and car for a couple of days; it was his anyway but she had taken possession of it. Things had seemed okay at first, but then a quarrel broke out as she did not want me to have use of these things. Phil had tried to get the keys from her bag, they were grabbling about on the floor, when her lip got knocked and started bleeding. Phil had run to get some tissue and whilst he was gone she had called the Police. When he came back his wife was sat on the floor, crying, surrounded by blood and the Police arrested him. "The Spanish police do not listen," he said, "they cuffed me, took me away in a van and I spent two nights in the cells. It was so degrading, I felt so shit. They let me out when the solicitor came." I, of course, felt so hurt for him.

After all of that was out of the way, we had the most fantastic night. The owner was putting some music together and Phil went over to talk to him. The next minute he was over by our table saying, "Your man tells me that you can sing. Would you be kind enough to sing for me?" We followed him out of the back doors and onto a balcony which looked over the wonderful outside restaurant. "Now please, sing." Well I could not say no so I sang my heart out! When I'd finished, he clapped and said, "You were wonderful. When I open this place in a few weeks, will you please sing for me? I will pay well. I have a waiter who is a rubbish waiter but he can sing, would you be willing to sing with him?" He was a very nice Egyptian man, "My name is Ahmed. I have many businesses and would like to invite you both to my private club on Friday evening. There we can drink and discuss, 'til then." He said as he kissed my hand and shook Phil's.

We went down the hill in excitement and happiness; it took about two hours to get home as we kept stopping. "Janette you always say the right things. Your love is incomparable to anything I have ever known." Phil said as he bent down, consumed me in his arms and kissed me. By the time we arrived home, we were exhausted and just fell into each other's arms.

Then it was another day. As anticipated we had a lovely relaxing day. In the evening Phil wanted to visit the pub in Alfaz where we first met. It was very romantic and we kept giggling about what we had said to each other. It was time to meet Ahmed so we took a taxi to his restaurant. From there he took us to a nice nightclub at the top of La Nucia. Ahmed was very generous to us and we were having a lovely time. "Oh God," I exclaimed, "My earring has fallen on the floor." A couple of people started to help to find it, including Ahmed. "Aren't you going to help, Phil?" I asked and his reply came, "You've got enough fucking people looking, including your boyfriend!" I couldn't believe how nasty he was being, but it was soon forgotten when he apologised. We went back to Phil's feeling tired and tiddly and happy; we fell into bed.

I woke up feeling happy. It was nearly lunchtime so I made Phil his first big cooked breakfast – including bacon cooked in honey, which he loved! We swam in his pool and had a lazy day; evening was upon us before we realised. It was barbecue night at his brother's so we got on our way to have a lovely evening. We stayed over and they just kept telling me how nice and fun I was and how happy Phil looked.

Chapter Seven

The next few days were spent having fun entertaining friends, plus Phil's brother and family. Walking, golfing and endless talking of things I had heard over and over from Phil, but I never lost interest. I had to support his unburdening. We were having such fun and love, and he told me constantly how I had given him more than he'd had in his life. Our love and bond grew day by day. The day before I was due to return to England, he begged me to stay, as he said he could not bear it without me; so I rang home and said I was stopping longer. There was a lot of upset but I wanted to be with him; so my heart ruled my head. So, we booked a flight for a later date; I paid as Phil was very tight on his income at this time. He had said he would reimburse me as soon as he got his money sorted (I'm still waiting).

On Friday 27th May 2011, I went into Old Benidorm to the lawyer with Phil. I sat in the waiting room when the lawyer came to me and said "Phil would like you to be in with him and myself, and does not want to go ahead 'til you are there please." So I followed him through. Phil was so pleased when I appeared and so the conversation began. At the close of the interview he said "I can help you Phil, but listening to everything you might as well have put a gun to your head." But after all, your solicitor is there to be on your side no matter what. After this we needed to unwind. It was getting late in the day so he took me to a place in Old Benidorm called *Vincent's*. We had a couple of drinks, and then Phil got up on the mike and sang *'When no one else can understand me.'* He was a good singer so it was very nice. We moved on to a very nice night club where we ate, drank, danced and had a lovely time. But all of a sudden Phil said "Let's go." His mood changed and we went back to his place in a cab. He was so argumentative when we returned; I stood my ground and he eventually went to bed saying "Just pack and get out." I slept on the sofa thinking "Well he's having a bad time." In the morning he came swiftly into the room (it was only 6.30 am) saying "Oh thank God you're still here, I did not mean it, don't ever leave me." I made coffee and we sat and chatted, then he picked me up and carried me to bed. Who could have predicted what later that day would befall us?

Later that afternoon, to my shock there was a terrible quarrel between Phil and a young man who I had never seen or met before. It was when we were at the top of the town in Alfaz having a coffee. Phil went round the corner to buy cigarettes, when after about ten minutes there was this dreadful shouting. One of the voices sounded like Phil's. Everyone was looking. I went to the corner to find Phil and a man shouting at each other. The young man was very tall and facing me said "Why don't you fuck off you ugly c***?" Shocked I realized this person was Phil's jealous son who'd had everything from Phil (as he had told me on so many occasions) and was now being offensive to me, whom he had never seen before. The realization hit home that he had taken our photographs as he still had access to the Villa. "Go on fuck off, why are you just stood there?" he continued. I never said a word but by now Phil was angry. There was a lot of tugging and shouting, then he pulled away and ran over to his car. Phil came and sat down explaining, "Oh that was my eldest son." He did not have to tell me, I had already gathered that. "I am so sorry, what a wicked, jealous son he is. Don't worry; we are big enough to get over it."

The next day we went golfing and just unwound. It was such a lovely day on the outskirts of Benidorm, up a hill. The evening was just as nice; I made a meal for Phil and his brother and family. We just ate, danced, drank, jumped in the pool, sang and everyone stayed. Once again they could not stop telling me how lovely I was and how happy Phil looked.

The day after, we had a lovely, long, uphill walk in the lovely, hot sun to a small town. It had a very interesting small factory which sold every kind of fresh honey you could care to desire; if only I could get a couple of barrels home, I could make a fair profit! We bought a very large jar for 5 Euros; it would have cost 50 Pounds in England! We had a lovely day but Phil decided that there was no way he could walk all that way back. I gently persuaded him to walk a little way down to the outskirts of the town; there we sat outside a nice pizza bar. The proprietor was very nice. He sat with us, chatting and refilling our glasses. We stayed a couple of hours then ordered a taxi back to

La Nucia to eat at Ahmed's Restaurant. I had first class treatment and how privileged I felt. Phil held me in his arms and we danced down the hill all the way home, surrounded by the beauty of scenery and each other. Soon we were home, falling into each other, encased in ecstasy. Tomorrow was going to be a bad day Phil felt, as he had to go to court in Alicante.

We borrowed a car and drove to Alicante the next day. Phil was so nervous but felt things would go okay; he had a good lady lawyer and she reassured him he would just get a fine. Waiting for him at court seemed endless, two hours was an eternity, but when he appeared he was relieved. "They fined me 1,000 Euros, which I have paid. She dropped the violence charges and was told she could not come to the villa."

"Oh thank God for you!" I replied. He kissed me gently and said "Thank-you, now lets get the hell out of here and on our way."

The next day was my last before flying home, and three days until Phil went back on the rig (the last thing he wanted to do.) We decided to go for a Spanish lunch. It was a rainy day but we walked all the three miles to the restaurant. Phil did not want me to go home, but everything was soon forgotten when the afternoon got underway. An English couple joined us; the afternoon was swinging and food and drink plentiful.

It was still raining when we decided to go, so a taxi was ordered for the four of us to go to Polop. Phil asked it to stop at a bar where he'd had a fling with the landlady. I thought, "This is a bad idea", but went along as he had promised not to get drunk, as he was driving me to the airport at 4 a.m. This was going to go so wrong that 'help' should have been the next word.

It was an unbelievable time once again. Phil sat playing chess at the bar and this woman kept climbing on the bar saying, "My eyes have won competitions, oh Phil I bought sexy shoes the other day, you would have loved it when I was running up the hill in them." Phil's brother appeared and the drinks were flying. Phil was telling me to kiss his brother to show him how I kiss him and how wonderful it was. "Not on your life Phil!" was my reaction. Then he was saying, "Go and kiss the man at the other end of the bar." This man had kept on asking me why I was with such an arsehole, but he himself was just like a slug, oh God help me.

Phil kept going outside for a cigarette and each time he would take me with him, kissing me passionately when the woman from the bar came outside. He was playing a game, punishing me because I was going back to England. It wasn't that I wanted to leave him, but I could not just leave things up in the air.

He was very drunk when we left; the woman kept looking in his eyes and telling him that she loved him. "Shit! What a cow!" I thought. Her husband had gone home earlier for the night. Phil's brother and I had such a struggle to get him home; he was falling in the bushes and pulling us with him. "Why?" What could I say? I could not be cross with him as he was just trying to stop me from leaving, but I knew he wouldn't be able to take me to the airport at 4 a.m.

In the villa, battered and bruised, we managed to get Phil to bed, with him calling in drunken tones "Remember my darling, I will get you to the airport." Phil's sister-in-law arrived in her little car and said she would get me to the airport, so I stopped panicking. We sat up talking 'til it was time to go. I slipped away quietly, kissing him on the cheek as he slept on, unaware. I was grateful to Phil's sister-in-law, but little did I know what a tyrant she would become towards me.

I arrived, checked in and was making my way for a coffee when my phone rang "Where are you?"

"At the airport, I could not let you bring me, but also could not wake you."

"I am fine; I wanted to be there with you."

"Sorry, I am missing you already"

"I love you, have a good flight. I will speak to you when you're back in England. I am just going to continue drinking to blot the thought of you not being here."

I arrived in England tired and missing Phil; I was picked up by a friend. Everyone was upset as it was half term and they had been relying on me, but that is the story of my life. In the evening Phil rang, what he was saying was illegible. The next thing I heard was another man's voice, "I'm afraid your boyfriend is very drunk, he hasn't stopped talking about how much he loves you all day. He is just drinking himself silly over how much he is missing you."

"Please put him to bed, I will call him tomorrow."

"I will."

"Thank you."

Next day I had my grandchildren and I told them about the nice things I had seen. We went out and had a lovely day. I cooked a roast for tea and they were pleased to stay in for the evening as we'd had a busy day. The phone rang and it was Phil, "Oh I can't bear it; the thought of going back on the rigs, so far away from you. I am so sorry; I just drank to block everything out. I have never felt this love before, please don't ever leave me."

"I won't, I love you so much. We are grown up adults and we will make it."

"Please will you call me early in the morning so I don't miss my flight?"

"Of course my darling, get a good night and I will call you in the morning."

"Kisses for you."

The next morning I woke early to call Phil. He was already up and so pleased to hear my voice. "Please come back, I won't go! Or shall I come to England?"

"Go and do your work, I will still be here when you get back and then we can make arrangements."

"Yes you're right. I love you Janette-Ann. I will call you as soon as I can. Hugs and kisses."

"Ditto."

If only we could have seen into the future; this story would not have gone on with passion, violence and threats of taking ones' lives!!!

Chapter Eight

The next few days were spent with family and friends – eating, talking and going to the races. I was very sad as I hadn't heard anything from Phil, but I was getting to know his make-up. Apparently this was Phil; how could I know someone so well when I had not been around him for long?

On the 13th May I was going to Market Rasen to stay with Phil's Mum. She had invited me and was so pleased to see me, but you never know people or what is round the corner! We sat in the kitchen talking and drinking tea and coffee most of the afternoon. The evening, I spent out with Phil's brother and family. It went well and we returned to find Vera still up.

On the 15th June we visited Brian's grave (Vera's deceased son); it would have been his birthday so Vera had taken flowers. He died of drugs Phil had told me, how sad! She also laid flowers at her husband's grave (Phil had told me stories about his Dad, not in the best of light, but I could not judge as I had not known him.) All I knew was Vera loved him; he was just a loveable rogue.

On the 16th June we went to Brough to visit Vera's youngest son who was in prison; no one would go with her and she was desperate to see him, so I took her. She was so happy. He was very pleasant; he asked me if I knew what I was doing getting involved with this family. Well it gave me food for thought but it did not last long. In the evening we went to Phil's brother's a few doors away from Vera's, and there it was, an email from Phil. That was all I needed; how happy it made me feel. Every worrying moment was forgiven. I returned to York the next day, happy I had been able to make Vera happy and to have heard from my love Phil.

Again I was home and had plenty to do. I saw my family and had my grandchildren to stay, sent emails to Phil and received them from him. I just wished he was there near me so I could give him the confidence he needed; God knows what shit he was getting via email from his son and Leanne. He told me in his email that he told Kyle to let her go back into the villa, as he would not be happy living there with me; he wanted somewhere fresh for us that was just ours, and we would start looking when he came home. I couldn't wait!

Life was busy with family and friends taking me out for lunch. But although I was missing Phil and hanging on to his emails, everyone said they enjoyed my company. I tried not to speak about Phil, but like most of the human race they would ask. I think it was mostly to fill their boring lives, as most people have found my life and personality great. But I have to admit; in the meantime my thoughts were on the new love in my life. Soon I was to be flying off to Spain to stay at my friend Connie's, while she was in England for three weeks looking after her pets. She had a lovely Spanish house on the edge of Alfaz; I love it there. Phil was going to come off the rig and stay while we got somewhere sorted for ourselves, I couldn't wait. I was blind to what July 2012 was going to turn into, help!

Connie picked me up from the airport and it was nice to see her. The next day she would be flying off early so we made the most of the day. During the evening we went to a bar called *The Park*, where all the Expat ladies meet; it had quite a few activities going on so it was nice. Next door was my favourite restaurant where I had been with Phil; the owner saw me and came out to give me a hug and kiss. He was so pleased to see me again, how lovely.

Next morning Connie was gone. I spent the next couple of days walking Frankie, going to see friends, swimming and sitting in the sun – what a life! On the Friday, Phil's sister-in-law asked me to go for the afternoon on the Saturday. Phil always called her the sister-in-law from hell, but I went and had a nice time. I got Frankie and went up to their home. I stayed and had a very nice weekend. I went down on Sunday morning to feed the cat then back to theirs' and had a fab day. They kept telling me what good company I was, and how lucky Phil was to have found me. They repeated over and over how happy he had been before he went back to sea, and realized he had never truly felt this love before.

Monday morning and Phil was due back, but I had no idea what his plans were for that day. Later that morning I received a call from Phil's brother "Phil's here. He's a little upset. He went straight to the villa to collect a few things but his wonderful son gave him a couple of black bags and threw him out." Who knows why? Who cares? My interest was just for Phil, the man who fell for me and me for him. I couldn't keep from loving him; my heart was so empty without him.

I took a cab up to his brother's. I walked in the room and saw a man slimmer than the last time I saw him. We stood and gazed at each other; the next minute we were in each others' arms, kissing like it was five years we had been apart, not five weeks. "I never knew kisses could be so wonderful, I have missed them so much. I love you Janette-Ann. I never want this to end my darling; it takes away all the terrible things that are happening". We sat out all the afternoon talking; or should I say Phil was. I listened, most things I had heard before, but what did it matter if it made him feel better? What had astounded him at the villa was Leanne telling Phil's brother how much she liked him; Phil had always thought she hated these in-laws because she said they had ruined their social life by coming to live there, and that she hated them with a vengeance. So it was another ploy of hers; God only knew what her gains would be. As Phil would say, he wasn't the brightest button in the box, so because of what Leanne said, he would try to turn Phil away from me.

The next few days were spent with Phil up in arms about everything and talking about the same things over and over; still I just listened and tried to make him feel safer. Then, when he got over his ranting, he would take me in his arms, kiss me and say "Come on, let's get out!" And off we would go walking, kissing and holding hands. Everything else did not matter for a while.

We had Connie's house to ourselves for three weeks, so that was lovely – or so I thought. Saturday came and Phil suggested going to his brother's to have a drink and play darts, so I went along. We arrived to find their friends were there; Phil had told me how undesirable they were some time before – the man owed him quite a lot of money. Well Phil went and sat at the bar and started talking to them as though they were long, lost friends. No one spoke to me for over half hour, so I took his sister-in-law to one side and asked if she would take me back down to Connie's. She was highly delighted to do so. I went without saying a word, as I knew Phil would persuade me to stay and I did not see any other answer. Phil did not ring me; he knew I had no money left as I had been helping out. My Spanish friends came round and we took the dogs for a walk and they gave me 20 Euros to get a few things, how kind of them that was.

On Sunday morning I still hadn't heard anything, so at 1 o'clock I called his brother. He said "Just get a taxi, we will pay. Bring the dog. You're like a couple of teenagers; he's moping here and you there." So off I went. I met Phil at the front, he paid then just held me, "Don't do that again, you know I hate it." He had stayed in all night unhappy while the others had gone out to see a singer. Why didn't he ring me? After all it was him that once again had put me in fear before I had even met them; why did he not see clear enough that he was the creator? Never mind. We had a nice afternoon swimming and walking the dog. In the evening we just cuddled on the sofa, him drifting in and out of sleep, and we stayed over. What a troubled man Phil was; could it be true what his Mother had told me – that he was a manic depressive?

We went back to Connie's in her car which she had loaned to us. Later in the day we went walking and stopped for a drink. He introduced me as his girlfriend to everyone he knew, then he would tell them every thing about what was going on with his life.

Chapter Nine

Later on we were very hungry, so we decided to go to the fantastic Chinese restaurant at the top of the town. We sat in the window. The lady owner always made a fuss of us; the only thing was that it was opposite where Darren (Phil's eldest son) worked at the bed shop. We ordered wine then just as we were looking at the menu, Phil went over to the shop. He came back rather upset, "I just asked him to come for a drink with us but he was just so impolite. Would you go over Janette my darling?" I refused, but he was so instant that he wanted us all to be friends. I was nothing to do with the breakup, it had been going on for years, so I went over against my judgement.

"What the fuck do you want?" was my greeting. But I kept my cool. "I have just come to say that I will leave the restaurant if you will come and have a drink and a civil word with your Dad. He has done so much for you."

"Get out or I will call the police. Who the fuck do you think you are? Fuck off." I left and returned to Phil.

"What did he say?"

"It doesn't matter, let's just eat and forget about him." But Phil was so insistent and everyone was looking. "He told me to fuck off." With that, Phil was gone and over the road. The next thing we all saw was a tall male throwing his Father in the road. Everyone in the restaurant was screaming. I ran over the main road to him. Phil was on his feet and now they were fighting. "Please stop!" I screamed, "How could you treat your Father that way?" He shouted some abuse and went off. I sat Phil on some steps and told him "Sit there while I go and apologise in the Chinese and get my bag." The people were disgusted with Phil's son and told me not to worry about anything.

We went round to the little church in the square and sat on the steps. Phil was battered and bruised and bleeding; it was so sad. The little place in the square where we went during the day had just closed, but the owner was still there and he brought us two glasses and a bottle of Cointreau.

"Please have, I will be pleased for you to have." How kind, we needed it. I wiped Phil's injuries with the cloths he had given to us and we just sat there in the warmth of the evening, holding each other, weeping and drinking.

Next day Phil slept until late, shell shocked about the whole situation. I was wondering why all this was happening, but my life always seems to be one dramatic episode after another. I made sure to tread very carefully as Phil was a total wreck. Later that day, in the early evening, we went into Albia. We had a lovely, long walk and talk. We drank lots of coffees and shared lots of kisses before returning home early. I tended to Phil's injuries then we cuddled on the sofa and watched a film. We both felt exhausted and slept like two babies that night, holding each other tight.

The next day we went for a drive after having early lunch at home. Phil wanted to go and see some cars as he wanted to go driving round the coast with the roof down. This was just one of the many things he had wanted do since living in Spain, but had always got knocked back by his wife. They were having a siesta at the car place, so we waited and fell asleep in the car. Phil was laid across my lap, relaxed and we drifted away. We woke at the rattle of the gates and both laughed out – we couldn't believe we had fallen fast asleep in the car. We made a move to go and see the lovely red Jeep that Phil had his eye on. The garage owner was German and he was very helpful. He said we were welcome to take it for a drive. Phil just loved it and the owner said he would hold it for a week. We came away feeling much better as Phil felt he had made headway, so after returning home, we got dressed up and went to our lovely Restaurant *Luncia Park* where we ate, sang and danced, feeling happy once again. We melted into each other's hearts that night. I was a lovely end to a lovely day.

The next day was just as lovely. Phil and I told of how much we loved each other. We drove to Calpe and sat all afternoon in two big, leather chairs at the front of a bar. We looked out at the sea, had a beer and didn't really talk – we did not need to; every time I turned to Phil he was looking at me and would just kiss me.

We decided to drive back to Alfaz. At the car Phil pulled me to him as we stood and said "I could have stayed there forever just sitting and looking at you. I just love to, you are so lovely." How lovely he made me feel.

We parked up in Alfaz, went to see our friends and went to *Robin's Nest* to see my favourite landlord and lady. Phil started playing chess and darts and I was happy to chat to everyone. I had a little game of darts with him, then who should appear? His brother. Phil had invited him, but that was the worst thing he could have done as he was not welcome at my friend's pub. The atmosphere was bad but I knew nothing about what had gone on. "There is a bad feeling, I will walk down to the car park with our kid; I won't be long." Once again the demon struck.

He was gone about half hour but I was quite happy on my own. "I cannot believe that is Phil's brother, he is not welcome here but you were not to know. He is very bad news and his other half is fucked in the head." Little did I know, she would be saying that about Phil in the near future, and other people I had yet to meet. It was getting late so we walked up to the square. We sat in the evening warmth and Phil went on and on about his brother. He decided he should distance himself from him and his wife as they had caused him so much trouble since their descent to Spain ten years ago.

When we got back in the house the tables were turned and I became Phil's target for two endless hours. He took a very nasty turn on me, going on about things I did not know about. I tried to hug him and calm him but he just pushed me away, saying "Don't touch me." He then started on about his wife, saying that I daren't ring her and I didn't respect her, then demanding "Ring her, ring her!"

"I don't know her and I was nothing to do with your break up."

"Who the fuck said you were? Just ring her!"

Had this man lost his marbles? He seemed to have gone crazy. I took the phone and rang her number, which was the old one in the villa "Hello it's Janette, would you like to have a talk with me?"

"Why the fuck would I want to talk to you after what you called my son?" I realized I was talking to yet another crazed person.

"What did she say?"

"Not a lot"

"Ring her back, get it done." How had I gotten into this again? I rang, saying "I thought you might like your husband back home"

"You having a laugh, why would I want that fucking thing back? I didn't want it long, long ago. Fuck off." She banged the phone down. "What did she say?" He was quite calm now. I told him the first words but not the latter. "I could have told you what she would say, that's about her limit brain wise. That was why I wanted you to ring, to realize how thick she is." My God was this really happening? "Come here on the sofa, I want to cuddle you, I want to tell you I am sorry." I did what he asked as I felt a little afraid – I have had a long history with a very violent man. He held me and kissed me and said "I have ruined a lovely day letting that trouble causing family in." It wound my insides up.

"It's not you darling," I felt calm, "I am tired, I would like to go to bed now okay." So off I went. Phil followed and we slept really well. What would tomorrow bring? It was becoming a nightmare!

It was as though nothing had happened the night before, except Phil repeated that we needed to distance ourselves from his brother and wife. It made no difference to me, as after all the things Phil had told me I thought it was the best thing he could do. Especially as he said they owed him money, plus they had borrowed 600 Pounds from his Mother when she had been over from England a few weeks previous for a holiday. We spent a quiet day just sitting out in the sun, having a bottle of wine and a few nibbles. "Come darling, let's get dressed up and go down town Friday night, make yourself beautiful as you always are." I had no idea how this night would end! When I came in the room Phil said "You are so beautiful Janette-Ann, I am so lucky." He stood up and held me tight, swinging me round the room. I felt so happy once again and off we went.

Chapter Ten

First we went to the square and sat outside. The owner took our order and when he returned he said "May I say how lovely you look tonight, as always."

"Thank you," Phil agreed, "But she is all mine." As we sat at the wine bar, a man named Brian, whom we had met a few days earlier, sat with us; he got the drinks and we had a nice chat. He was going home the next day and was on a heartbreak holiday as his lady-friend (who was fifteen years his senior) had told him she wanted to end their relationship and spend more time with her grandchildren. I wish I could have met her and given her some advice about doing this – you lose your grandchildren in this modern day, no matter how good you have been, and she was breaking this man's heart, who would have loved to share life with her. Well that's my advice for what its worth.

I had to go to the ladies' but when I returned, Brian had gone. I was surprised as Phil had said he could move on to the next place with us. "Where has he gone? Did he decide to be on his own?"

"No. He said he didn't realize how beautiful my wife was – assuming. I told him it was time he moved on, you're mine, and not to get any silly ideas."

"How embarrassing Phil, you should have just accepted it as complimentary; I am not a piece of property."

"Sorry darling, but I just get jealous when I know other men are interested. We all went 'woo' when we saw you coming, you're the best thing we've seen in Alfaz." Well the compliments were nice, but I could see Phil was not liking it; still, he got attention from women but I didn't make a fuss as I knew he would be going home with me. As the drinks flowed, we decided to move on. A man called Kyle invited us back to his villa but Phil declined. He gave me his telephone number as they were having a jazz band at their home on Sunday and a 'barbie' round the pool; he said he would love for us to go, "You will be made very welcome." He bent over and kissed my cheek. "I want you, and the man you are with is a well-known arsehole. Please ring me." Well I did not take heed of what he said as I was so in love with Phil.

We went to *Robin's Nest* next. "Getting more than your share of attention tonight, not surprising as you are so lovely." said Phil. At the pub Phil met the landlord of *The 19th Hole*. I found him to be very bolshie so I had no interest in being in his company, but Phil was asking him lots of questions. I felt he was Leanne's friend, but it made no difference to me, I was nothing to do with anything that had gone on before.

We decided to walk home. We were only half way home and it was a very lonely area, but still Phil said, "You go on home, I am going to *19th Hole* to get to bottom of this."

"So you're leaving me alone at 12.30 a.m. to be on my own?" With that he was gone, so I hurried on back home, looking round all the time. It took me about ten more minutes as I was hurrying. I got back and Frankie was so pleased to see me. I locked the door and was about to go straight to bed when there was a knocking on the door. I called, "Who is it?"

"Who do you think? Don't be stupid."

"Why don't you go back to where you went when you left me to find my own way home?" Still, I opened the door. He went straight to the kitchen, got four bottles of red wine, two glasses and took them to the front. He said, "Get yourself out here." I should have just locked him out, and I would if I had known what was about to be a very frightening two hours. He opened a bottle of wine and poured two large glasses out. We were just drinking. I asked, "Would you like something to nibble with our drink?"

"No just sit there where I can look at you." His face was so frightening. With anger, after his third drink, he started on me verbally. He never left me alone. "Why don't you fuck off to your rich boyfriends'?" He mentioned four people we had come to be friends with; they were restaurant owners and Phil had introduced me to them all. He had even put me in the position of being asked to sing in one of the places on Saturday evenings over summer. He was shouting, "We're not going to any barbeque on Sunday! Why don't you go and fuck your boyfriend?" Ashamed, I was very frightened. Although the police had the first house in the cul-de-sac I could not get away from him, and I did not really want to have Spanish police on him as he'd had Leanne on his back with them. I decided to retaliate, whatever were the outcome, "I haven't done anything Phil, but I do know you embarrassed me with the landlady in Polop! Also with the one from the pub the night before I went home in May, when your sister-in-law implied you had been having an affair with her."

"Do you mean a sexual affair while I have been with you?"

"Well what would you think?" Well Phil went mad, shouting, "Did she say I was fucking her?" He said it over and over then jumped up and had a pee in the corner of the front garden. I took my chance. I ran in, locked the door and went in the kitchen where I got a knife. By now he was banging and shouting at the door. I stood by the window with the knife near my heart saying "If you don't stop I will put this in me, I cannot take anymore."

"Let me in please, I will behave. I have been out of order. Please, please don't do any thing silly. It's not you." So I relented and let him in; what a mistake. "You're going to stab me." I really thought he was really crazy. "Of course not, I would not hurt you or anyone. I did not know what to do to stop you."

I put the knife back in the kitchen. With that, Phil went running out of the back door to the end of the long garden where there was a steel door with a bolster lock. It opened easy, but no, Phil climbed over the wall tearing his new top. He was crazy. I just sat down. I did not know how I felt. My body felt like it had been wrecked. Before I knew it, there he was, back standing in front of me. "Please sit outside, have a relaxing drink." I made a coffee and Phil continued with the wine but he seemed calmer.

We decided to go in so I locked up. Then Phil became passionate but with aggression; he pulled me to the bedroom and started on a very long, abusive sexual stint saying "I want to love you, I want to hurt you." I knew the best thing to do was to go along with him. I had seen him in a sexual hurting place before, but nothing on this level. After he fell asleep every part of my body was hurting and parts were even bleeding. The pain in my back was unbelievable. Oh God what was happening? I should have rung for a taxi to take me to hospital but I just lay there wondering what to do. This man I had fallen in love with was unstable! I did not sleep well, just drifting in and out of sleep. I was in pain and worrying about what was going to happen to both of us. It was too much to bear but I drifted off for a couple of hours.

Phil slept while 1 o'clock then he got up. He had a black coffee, washed and shaved and put a few thing in a bag before saying, "I am leaving. I don't know where I'm going." But it didn't take much working out. "Please don't walk out without working something out with me. I don't feel well and need you here with me."

"Well I would really like to stay with you my lovely woman." He got up and took Connie's keys, "Where are you going with those keys? You don't take that car without me. It was loaned to me for you to take us about."

"I am going to put fuel in and clean it." I knew differently. He would be sneaking up to brothers' to give him the gossip. "I shall be back in a couple of hours."

"I feel so poorly Phil."

"Well have a lay down." How cold and cruel he was. I cried as he went, but pulled myself together. I cleared the mess up, had a shower, washed my hair and changed. My private places were bleeding so I made myself as comfortable as I could and laid outside in the sunshine for an hour; Frankie never left my side. After a while I went in and drank some water. Then I laid on the bed with a couple of paracetamol and Frankie at my side; how I needed this. Well Phil's two hours turned into five hours. I woke at 4 p.m. to find him not back. 5.30 came and he appeared in not a very nice mood. He had been drinking with the evil ones (his brother and sister-in-law) He threw 300 Euros on the table. "That is what you are getting. I have put in 60 Euros of fuel."

"Well you have had the car for two weeks and I had it half full before you arrived. Plus Connie did not expect you to pay the rent on the house but you told her on the phone you would, which is 500 Euros you know. I have already paid her bills and bought things in the house and should be staying longer with you; so what am I supposed to do?"

"Why are you being like this?"

"You have done this awful thing to me. I am feeling so poorly with it."

"I have asked my sister-in-law if she said those things about me and Jerella. She said you are a liar and you are just after my money."

"Well that takes the biscuit! What money?" I hadn't seen any of it. That was my last thought seeing as he still owed me for last May. Was this the horror he had talked about to me, saying at times he couldn't lay straight in bed with all the trouble they had caused him, and telling me she fancied him, which was quite apparent! Even still they owe him money; how their wicked weave spins. I put my arms round his neck, "Please don't leave. Sort this out with me. I need to get treatment for the pain I am in." He pushed me away, "I have to go."

"Oh are they waiting for you on the main road? – The people who you said we must distance ourselves from?"

"What has happened to the woman I met and fell for at the start of this year?"

"It's called Phil Higgins. You are so weak. Just go, I have survived in my life without your kind. My heart is still full of you, but you have no compassion." With that he was gone. I just sat and thought, "What do I do now?" But right at this moment in time I felt too poorly to even think.

Later that evening I took the lovely, sweetheart dog for a little walk. He was so sweet; he had been growling at Phil the night before – well done Frankie! We did not go far as I felt so faint. When I returned, I called a friend to see if they would take me to the walk in centre; they came and could not believe how poorly I looked. At the centre they gave me tablets and soothing cream for my personal parts. They asked me lots of questions, but I was reluctant to answer because I did not want to get Phil involved with the Police. My friend took me home and I said "I will be okay now; I will call you if I need you. Enjoy your wedding party." It was after 10 p.m. and I decided to ring Phil. He answered and was having a good time by the sound of it, "Hello Janette. Why don't you come?" I thought it pointless to tell him anything. I heard a familiar voice say, "Who is it?"

"Oh it's Janette." With that I put the phone down. "You bastard!" was my thought. How could he be out enjoying himself with the evil ones and not even have the decency to call me? I never heard a thing all day Sunday. I knew I would have to get home as I was getting worse.

That evening I walked down to the internet cafe where I booked a flight home for early Tuesday morning; this cost 165 Pounds but I had to do it. There was no word from Phil. I tried his phone but it seemed to be turned off.

Monday came and still there was no word. I booked my taxi for the early hours of Tuesday – 45 Euros, the costs were endless. I was sad as I had always been happy there and loved going to my friends', but I was feeling worse by the hour. I put 170 Euros in an envelope for my friend. I had nothing left in the bank, I just left myself 20 Euros for a drink at the airport. I didn't need more as a friend was picking me up in England. "What is going on once again in my life?" I thought.

I arrived at my home around 10 a.m. and ran a bath. My friend had a drink then had to get off to work. Here I was in bewilderment: crying, hurting in my heart and in my body. Oh God. I laid on the bed and was woken about 12.30 p.m. by my phone; it was Phil. "Where are you? I am just going into court; I have been locked up since Saturday evening. I went to the villa and her and that arsehole son had the police on me. I want you here at my side."

"I'm afraid that is impossible."

"I will call you when I come out if they don't lock me up." How did he think people ticked? Within an hour he was back on the phone. "They were going to lock me up or give a 3,500 Euro fine, so I paid the fine. Where can we meet? I need to see you."

"I am at home in England. What else could I do?"

"I cannot believe it."

I put the phone down. So much for the man with no money, and who left me in the predicament I was in – hurting physically and mentally and my heart beating at a thousand beats. What had I done to this man except brought him back into life and loved him? And he kept saying constantly that he realized he had never been loved in his life.

On Wednesday there was no word from Phil as he'd promised; well what did his promises mean? Not a lot. I think this man drives you to heaven then takes you to hell. He was so righteous, always expecting me to accept everything. Even through the drink motivated visits to his villa which were encouraged by others, this was what cost him his freedom and money.

On Saturday I had my darling granddaughter to stay. We went for something to eat and had a lovely time. She was picked up the next day; how I love having her round. A friend came to see me and we had some nibbles and a laugh so it was nice; then phone rang. It was Phil. My friend went as she had to get home; good job as he was on the phone over two hours saying how sorry he was, how he hated everything without me, how much he loved me and if I would forgive him he wanted to book a flight to York and come and stay so we could sort everything out. Of course my reply was yes. How much I loved this man. I came of the phone feeling so elated but would not rely on anything till I saw him stood at my door.

Chapter Eleven

Next day Connie arrived from Spain; she was staying a few days, then going to see her various family, then coming back. So it was hectic but nice to have her here. My son came for tea so it was nice; we all enjoyed our evening. I kept chattering about Phil coming to York.

On Wednesday 9th August, my Aunty in Bath died. She was the youngest sister of my darling Mum, so it was sad. The next call I had was Phil, from Spain "Hello darling. I am calling to say I need to work to get some money together for us, so I will not be coming to York. I will be setting off for the rig on Sunday."

"But you had already decided that you wanted to come to York to see me and make things right before you went. How easily you are tempted and swayed by others. You are so weak; you're making my heart ache again." I started to cry.

"Please don't. We will have lots of time when I return and we can see to our own place in Spain." I could not speak so he said "I will call you later." Well we all know what that means by now. Connie went off to the hairdresser's saying "I feel so hurt for you." What can I say? I dried my eyes.

We came back to my house and Connie went off in the car to see her daughter for a couple of days. It was a sad evening, I didn't hear from Phil. After talking to my cousin in Bath I just put myself to bed and cried myself to sleep.

Next day, 10th August was my grandson's birthday, so that was nice. It would also have been my wedding anniversary with the Father of my four wonderful children. But then, shock upon shock, I had a call from Beverley town telling me that my Uncle had passed away – Mum's younger brother. It was all so bizarre and sad. No call from Phil. "Spineless creature" I thought. So I spent a lonely and sad night talking to my relations. It will soon be tomorrow, see what that will bring; but my head was spinning and my heart was heavy; finding sleep was hard.

I was met with pain in every part of my body when I woke. I went to my G.P as I had been suffering for a while. My results had come back; I had a kidney problem and had to start on treatment. But I knew something nasty was going on, I had just felt worse and worse over the past two weeks but was trying to cover it up; what crazy things we do when we love someone. I just wanted this love to work. Will I never learn? This problem was mine and it was not going to hurt anyone but me. The future has proved different, but there is more to tell!

Walking round golf courses in Spain was a pleasure; apart from Phil's constant talk about Leanne – how she had showed him up this, that, constant, same. Then about the abusive son. After about two hours it would stop, and then we would go and have a pleasurable day. My love never wavered from him, but I was having doubts about his state of mind; little did I know this would stress me and make me so poorly as to cost me part of my sight. Even in Market Rasen we would play golf with his brothers. That was very cold, but for me it was a respite as I would have a giggle with his brothers, so it veered away from Phil's repeated complaining!

We had a few nice days Connie and I. My grandchildren came to stay on the Friday evening and we went to my favourite Indian. Everyone enjoyed it. The restaurant owner knew me well as it was the only Indian I went to, because it was delicious. I had taken Phil there earlier in the year as he loved Indian food, and he was more than pleased with it. "Where is your friend Janette-Ann?"

"In Spain."

"Best place for him. I feel wrong things about him."

"How perceptive" I thought!

Morning came and Jack had to go to play in his team. Jill made a breakfast menu for Connie (how sweet.) Connie could not believe such a lovely thing; it was delivered to her bedroom on a tray. Soon she was up and on her way back to Spain; she left a tip on the tray for her wonderful waitress. A nice time was had by all. Connie hugged me, "Please take care with that man, and I will be in touch. See you in September."

On the evening of Saturday 13th September my phone rang. When I answered it was Phil's Mum, what she told me made me laugh for hours, "While Phil was out walking and drinking all day (as he was staying with the brother) they were out at work and the two dogs which they left all day of course were bored, and one of them had got Phil's passport and chewed it up." His Mother was going on about how much she never liked that dog, but I was in fits of laughter. "He is having to go to Glasgow to renew it; the office is only open Saturday morning. So he is hanging on by his breath as he's due out in the early hours of Monday morning to the Black Sea on the rig."

I was realising now that's where he belonged. I had to get off the phone as I could not speak for laughing (serves him right.)

I got a call on the Saturday night from Phil telling me all about it. I could not believe he had been so stupid as to go all the way back to Spain for a few hours, when he had said he had his bag all packed and he would be flying from England. "Where could I have gone?"

"Well you could have stayed in a B&B for a night, or if you had to wait a few days you could have come and settled a few matters with me."

"That's what I wanted to do, but I was so afraid you wouldn't forgive me."

"What a load of bunkum. You wanted to go back to being the centre of attention; telling your story and having a full day drinking with those you had wanted to distance yourself from."

Chapter Twelve

The week following was all hustle and bustle; teas out, four little angels staying (eating me out of house and home), tea with my sister and two funerals (how sad; my lovely Mum's sister and brother.) And with all the support I had given Phil, not a word from him. What an absolute arsehole; he made me so cross!

At my Aunty's funeral in Bath I was sad thinking about her and her family. The next day I would attend my Uncle Lesley's funeral in Willoughby – sad, but lovely to see my cousins and especially my cousin from Dubai.

The next day I had a lovely time at the races where I met a fantastic group of men – Lord Phillip and sons. I brought them home where we sat in the garden laughing, singing, dancing, drinking and eating. I think this was the end to rather a fruitful week. It started to rain so we sat under umbrellas as two of them smoked; but it was warm so it was fun. I ordered taxis for them then went to lay on my bed to listen to my music. I was so wrecked I just fell into a sleep, with Phil in my ear asking me to forgive him. My company, I remember them calling "Good night, our cab's here", locked up!

The next I knew it was 8 a.m. I dashed down stairs to find everything okay, but I was feeling rather under the weather so I had my *Andrews* and went back to lay down and think about how let down I felt with Phil's behaviour.

I went to Phil's Mum's for a few days. Phil got in touch via his sister-in-law's laptop but he did not have a lot to say, except that he felt low, loved me, and was sorry and confused. Well how did he think I felt knowing he was on the rig depressed? I returned home and a day later my new laptop arrived (hurrah); now I could send my own things!

On the 10th September it was my young grandson's wedding. How lovely they looked; how wonderful everyone else looked. I just longed for Phil to be at my side for such a lovely occasion. Why did this never happen for me? It seemed I gave so much to this man and got nothing back, but this has always seemed to be a pattern in my life. Never mind, I was there with my lovely family and it was fantastic to see all my grandchildren so smart (whooooooooooo!)

Next I went to a fantastic barbeque at my son and daughter-in-law's for the parents and grandparents of the happy couple. I sang for them before they went off on their wonderful honeymoon. I came home and sent an email to Phil, but it was days before he replied. He was just going on about himself again and sending me yet again all the nasty emails his family had sent, "So you can see why I am depressed getting all this shit."

"Well why try? It has cost you dearly. Just keep a low profile and just deal with your reasonable son although you're not too happy with him." He was not happy about any of this, so he went into his 'manic mode' as his Mother would say to me on the phone. I had lots to fill my life and just got on with it; although my heart was constantly beating at 500 hundred fathoms, pining for Phil as never had we closed our love.

On the 25th September I was to fly back to Spain. Phil sent me a short message saying he loved me and he would be there when I was there, so let's see what will happen!!!

I went back to my favourite place, Alfaz. Connie picked me up from the airport and it was nice to see her again. On Monday Connie went to work; I was tired so slept a lot during the morning, but I kept waking and wondering about Phil. Connie came home in the evening, and then I took Frankie for a walk while she had a little rest. At night we went out and got very drunk; I have got to say, I felt very poorly the next day.

Phil was back, but yet again he had been stupid; he was a hair's breadth away from getting locked up. He said he did long to see me and talk about things, so we made a date for the Friday at 8 p.m. We were having a trip to Denia during the day on the train. It was a lovely journey, and Connie had always wanted to do it with her Mother, but she had died suddenly the year before so never had the chance. So, it was nice for Connie. I am afraid my tummy was so giddy for meeting Phil at night; I never visited so many loos in one city. On the journey back I had to ring Phil to say we would be a little bit later, "Don't worry darling, I am just going down to Alfaz myself. I need to collect some money. See you soon." I kept asking Connie if I looked okay,

"You look lovely, stop worrying." As we went up town to our meeting place I saw Phil come out of a side street.

My heart was thumping as I called his name. He turned, and it was just like a film. We ran into each other's arms; him lifting me and just kissing and kissing me. "How I have missed you."

"And me you."

"I love you Janette." We remembered Connie was stood there, so we went round the corner to the lovely wine bar and sat outside on the lovely white tables and chairs. Phil ordered nice wine, nibbles and chocolates. I sat close to Phil and drank my wine. After a couple of drinks, Connie said her goodnight and left us as we had so much to talk about. After a couple of hours (which seemed to fly) I asked if he would see me back to Connie's, "No you're staying with me. I told you I have been busy all day and I have things to show you." The next minute we were in a taxi going up to La Nucia. Phil took me through these big gates into a complex of houses; he had rented a house, so that's where I found myself, sitting on the porch, drinking wine with the man I loved dearly. It was still warm so we made good use of such precious times; kissing gently and passionately, filling all those times we had missed and wasted. If only he could keep this momentum and build on it, instead of being weak and led away by mindless people. I fell asleep in his caresses; so happy to be near him and he near me. Tomorrow is another day.

I woke early the next day and went down to sit in the sun with a relaxing pot of tea; Phil was still sleeping. The time flew and Phil appeared, desperately wanting his morning coffee. We sat in the porch most of the morning, talking and drinking our tea and coffee. Phil spoke about endless things; most I'd heard before, some I hadn't. But the most important thing was that he wanted this love between us. We had a very relaxing day with just one interruption – some undesirable company; but never mind, I was with the man I loved. That evening we took a ride into Albir, had a lovely walk in the evening then returned to Phils; heaven was back again.

On Sunday Phil went to play golf and I wanted to see Connie, so he paid for my taxi to Alfaz Del Pi. We walked and talked, then later on we ate at a posh restaurant after a yummy cake competition had finished. I stayed at Connie's that night and the next day I spoke to Phil; he was very low again and had to go to pay a 2000 Euro fine. He was going on about how he didn't like where he was living. He was too near to the very people who caused him trouble (he is so hoodwinked by these people, how sad!) He makes me so cross; he moans about money and then does silly things. Phil was low again so I did not go back. That evening he called me and talked about our future and said he wanted to make arrangements to meet for tea the next day in Alfaz. I went to sleep feeling happy, but sad that he has this low feeling again.

The next day I could not wait to see him. I went for a lovely swim at the outdoor sports centre in Alfaz, then hurried back to get ready to meet Phil. Up in the town I got a million phone calls from Phil (well maybe just ten) telling me that he was near, but was getting surprises for me and so not to worry. All of a sudden, I caught sight of him coming up the street, his arms full. I waved from where I was sat; it seemed to be an age before he got to me. He was holding the most beautiful bouquet of deep red roses, "These are for you, to say how much I love and appreciate you. You are so lovely and deserve to be treated with a lot more than I am giving at this time, but I will make it up to you!"

"Don't worry, you will see it all in a different light soon." I was living in hope of course! We went to eat at the lovely Chinese restaurant, and then went back to Phil's. It was sweet heaven again; sat on the porch holding hands and falling asleep in the warm night air. We woke and Phil took me up to bed.

The next day it was go time. He had to be off early to meet up with a group he had joined to play golf. He left money for me to go to Alfaz to shop and see my friends, saying he would be home around 5.15 p.m. He seemed so happy, a natural happening. I cooked a nice chicken dinner, but was losing heart. At 6.15 p.m. he rang and said "I will be their shortly."

"Okay." When he arrived home at 6.30 p.m. he could not believe I was not cross, "I am not yet used to your lovely attitude. You have made a lovely meal, but will it keep 'til tomorrow? I want to take you to Albia. We have lots of time in the future to do these things." He didn't have to ask twice; I was ready in a flash. He had showered at the club, so quickly changed and ordered a taxi. We had a glass of wine on the porch whilst waiting. I felt so lucky; this is all I wanted to make my life complete. All I had longed for; he and I, my lovely children and grandchildren.

We arrived in Albia and took a nice evening walk along the beach front. Phil didn't do sand, but that didn't matter; just being here holding hands, kissing gently and passionately, feeling the warmth and closeness of each other. We found ourselves at the *Coca-Cola* bar and restaurant. Phil was feeling hungry so we ordered wine and mussels. It was dusk so we sat outside the bar in the musky, warm evening. There was only one other person sat a few tables away, so we sat on a chair together and made the night explode. "What is happening to us Phil?"

"Everything is wonderful. I never thought I could feel, or did not know you could feel like this. Let's pay the bill and go home and hold each other all night and forever." How wonderful I felt. How lucky I was; never did this feeling ever feel stronger.

Then it was my birthday. Phil gave me money as my girlfriends were going for lunch with me at the Spanish restaurant in Alfaz. We arranged to go to Benidorm in the evening to have a lovely dance and celebrate my birthday, so I was feeling on top of the world. We had such a lovely day and returned to Connie's to have a siesta. I was so high I just sat on the balcony and drank coffee.

Evening came and I was so looking forward to Phil coming. I was all prettied up and it was half an hour past his time to pick me up, but that was nothing out of the norm for him. I waited a little longer then called him; he sounded low and as if he had been drinking. His words just broke me up again, "I am not coming. I feel too low and have been thinking all day. I have wanted to buy you a ring and all these things are going on in my head."

"Please don't do this to me; it's my birthday. I am going back to England in the early hours of Sunday. Please, please come and have fun. Don't keep punishing us. Who have you been with today? Need I ask? Giving you unwanted advice. I know you Phil; don't listen to all that shit. Can't you see these people are jealous and want what we have got? So if they see you are weak enough to listen to them they will always go for the jugular."

"You go enjoy yourself with your friends. I am feeling really shitty and low. I love you, but don't know where I am going." I put the phone down. I wanted to cry and scream but I didn't. "I knew he wouldn't come when he had been at the mercy of that lot up there! Well come on, we're still going out!" I jumped up and shouted. "Yes let's go get wrecked and dance the night away." So soon we were flying off in a cab to Benidorm. We went from place to place, dancing, singing, drinking; I even sat and ate chips and peas in the square. My phone rang, "I should have come, and I should not take notice of these people up here. I am so weak."

"Phil I am too wrecked to even talk, so good night. We are just falling in a cab to go home to Connie's." The ride home I did not remember, except I felt very sick and everything was swimming. I went straight to my bed; I remember hearing my phone ringing but did not have the strength to answer. I was consumed with drink and emotion.

The next day I spent mostly laying around drinking water, taking paracetamol and not answering my phone. The next day I would be on my way again; on my own it would seem. Phil had said he would come to York with me and we would go forward, but somehow I didn't see this happening!

Chapter Thirteen

Once again, I was on my way home without the man I was waiting for. At boarding time my phone went, "Where are you?" That question once again. "Wait for me?"

"I can't trust that you will come and I can't come back. You will know where I am. I feel so let down, stressed and poorly."

"I will be in York this following weekend, please wait for me there? I won't let you down. I can't wait for this week to go."

"So I will wait and see. Seeing is believing. Bye my love."

"Don't leave, I love you." My heart was so heavy to leave, but what could I do? Up 'til now this year with Phil was filled with disappointment, jealousy to the point of physical and mental stress, heartache for no reason. I can say I have loved him and supported him throughout it, only to keep getting let down time after time.

Monday 10th October was a busy day at home and out and about. I wrote letters. Phil's family was coming at the weekend to York and his Mother was staying for a few days. Phil and I text each other; the conversation was lovely between us. He was very confident about coming. He was missing me and I him. He was saying for sometime that he had to have a refresher survival day and could do it whilst here, so things seemed promising.

My lovely granddaughter came to stay Friday and Saturday. We had a lovely time but it was soon gone and she went home at teatime (how I love these times.)

On Sunday morning at 11 o'clock, the front door went. I had made nice fresh scones for my company. As I opened the door, I was met by Matt, his wife and Phil's Mum Vera – no Phil. My heart dropped. Matt was so lovely, "Don't look so worried; he has arrived but is catching up with Dennis and will be here tomorrow." Well we would see.

We had a lovely day; Sharon and I went to *Designer Outlet* and Matt took his Mum to York to see a couple of sights. We met up with them and went to *Plonkers* for a meal. Back at my house, Phil's Mum stayed and Matt and Sharon got on their way back home. We had a very chatty night but never heard from Phil. His Mother told me about four times that Phil was not coming; every time it felt like a knife through my heart. After all he surely would let me know?

Next morning I had to go to the bank, "Will you be okay on your own while I pop to town?"

"Of course." Little did I know just how okay! I was back within an hour. It was a nice day outside so I said I would take her out after lunch. I was feeling so hurt but tried not to show it. Then there was a knock at the door. I opened it to see Phil stood there. My heart did three somersaults. "Your Mum said you weren't coming."

"Why did she say that?"

"She's here, why don't you ask? But really it doesn't matter. You're here and that's all I care about." We fell into each other's arms and kissed until we could not breathe. "You said you weren't coming" was the call from his Mum.

"I said, tell Janette I will be there on Monday. That's why I didn't ring; I thought she would be expecting me."

"You're here, so let's have a super time."

"Well said darling. I have hired this nice car, so let's get going."

"Sounds good to me." We took his Mum with us of course. We parked up and went to the York museum. We thoroughly enjoyed every minute; three hours seemed to fly. Phil and I were holding hands and helping his mum. He kept kissing me gently on the back of the neck; we actually got through a full day without reference to Leanne. In all their years he always wanted to do these things, but she never would. Well I felt that this was the break through at last.

In the evening we went to my favourite Indian restaurant as Phil loved the food, "That was one of the nicest Indian meals I have had. Good choice darling." We walked home and it was a pleasant evening. Our twenty minute walk took two and a half hours – well there were more stops than starts, loving and kissing in abundance. When we finally reached home, I was floating. Phil said he felt like a jelly. We opened the door to find Vera still up, "Now then Mother, why are you still up? It's nearly 1 a.m." Well I realize now why only too late you think people are your friends, but a lot of the time it is just a plan and when it comes it is a hurtful shock. The elderly are especially vindictive with their jealousy; they have had longer to practice and plan. Phil went up to bed calling, "Darling, are you coming to bed? I have to go on the course tomorrow teatime and won't be back 'til Thursday teatime." So I got Vera up and went and snuggled in my lovely round bed with my love. Always the optimist.

Next day the hours went quickly to the time Phil was leaving me to go on his course in Middlesbrough. Afternoon came and he was gone with a kiss and a wave, "I love you, see you in two days. Can't wait to return." He was gone and I always feel so uncertain when we part, as I have every good reason to. He is strong in so many ways but he is weak in other matters, led by uncertainties in his own mind.

Early evening came and Phil was on his third call "I hate this place and missing you is making me hate it more. I have decided to take your advice and I'm going to see a film. Please will you book theatre tickets for Friday night and we will go and have a lovely evening. This is just the beginning of many things I long to do with you, to add to the things we have done already. You have always made them so wonderful and I have acted so badly. But it is going to change. I have felt so frightened as I never felt this before for a woman. It did not feel real. I will call you when I get out of the film. Love for now." Oh how happy I felt at this moment. True to his word, he rang after the pictures. He was trying not to drink as he had under water survival the next day. I told him what was on at the theatre, "You choose darling, whatever. I will be with you." Oh had heaven reached me at last?

The next day I booked the theatre to see *Laurel and*

Hardy; for three as we were taking his Mum. It was a busy day; I took Vera to see the walls. I walked her a little way as it was easy to get on at *Lendal Bridge*. We sat on a seat with the sun shining; it was so lovely. She loved it, said I was so good and caring. I called a cab to take us home as it was nearing teatime and Vera had done enough for the day. The phone went just as we finished tea "Hi darling, have you booked the theatre?"

"Yes, for three to see *Laurel and Hardy*. I thought it would be nice to take your Mum. I hope it will be a good performance."

"I am sure it will be, but as long as I am with you it doesn't matter."

"Well all these things I am pleased to hear and feel I have such warmth running through my heart."

"I will call to say goodnight. I'm going for a curry and a pint. Love for now darling, lots of kisses." As promised he called to say goodnight. When in charge of his own mind he is so wonderful, or that's how it felt. "One more day and I will be homeward to you. My life is so different with you. I want to start treating you the way you deserve. I know I have not a lot of the time. I have been so frightened of this love you have shown me and I have felt. All my love, goodnight."

On Thursday my son came and gave us a lift so we could take Phil's Mum to the Minster. She was pleased as she could not walk a lot. The trip into the minster was wonderful for her as she could keep sitting then doing a little more. "I am so grateful to come and experience this wonderful place. It has been yet another wonderful day." We made our way home in a taxi and then it was tea time.

Phil rang to say he had a very hard day and was going early to bed, to be home as soon as possible into my loving arms. He was also looking forward to the theatre. We said our sweet talks, exchanged kisses and then he was gone.

The next day was endless waiting for Phil to arrive back. It was so lovely to have him close again as for the past few days he had been the man that I met, liked, and fell in love with.

Going to see *Laurel and Hardy* at the theatre couldn't have been better; it was excellent. We put Phil's mum in a taxi home, as we wanted to stay out to have some time together and a drink. I know we stayed out rather late and I had more than my share of wine. I took Phil to a few pubs in York which have character; he really loved it, "I would live here with you. How we all lived our young life in Owersby I will never know, and it is the last place I would ever want to live".

Chapter Fourteen

At lunch time the next day, we were on our way to take Vera back to Owersby. She said she'd had a lovely time and had been well looked after. We were soon back to Market Rasen and Phil's Mum's. She was glad to be home as she had not walked so much for a long time, but had loved it. Cups of tea were had all round and there was lots of chatter, as Matt came round. "Would you like to go out this evening with Graham and myself?" Phil was all for that. We went for a drive into town, a drink and a walk holding hands; we felt so at one. The evening was unbelievable; for a Saturday it was like a ghost town. We weren't late home, "Goodnight Matt. Thank you. See you in the morning for golf."

"You're home early."

"Yes we're tired and are going to bed." Phil was feeling the strain, as we had not stopped since his return from the course, so sleep was soon upon us.

I was woken at about 3 a.m. by Phil "Let's go down and have a drink and a little chatter love." So we went into the kitchen, opened a bottle of red wine and thoroughly enjoyed every minute of the next two-and-a-quarter hours.

Phil was telling me all of the wonderful things I wanted to hear; how his loved had grown for me and he knew where he was going now. Sitting on his knee, I felt like a young woman with all his kisses and caresses. It was as if we were the only two people in the world. We crawled upstairs and fell into a heavenly sleep in each other's arms and minds.

Earlier that day we had all gone for a meal at a restaurant where everyone moaned constantly that Phil and I were too loved up to care; it was a total headache. I had never before been in a group where all complained. In the end I went myself to tell the staff that the group were not happy, but Phil and I were pleased with our food. We had risotto!

The next day was spent walking, shopping and cooking. I made a nice meal, we watched television and had an early night. I felt so happy and close. Through the night I was woken up again and Phil suggested we went downstairs. I had come to accept, and like, that he often used to wake me and like us to get up and talk and get loved up and have a drink leisurely. We had only been down ten minutes when his mother appeared. She had commented to me that morning about how she thought we had been up through the night as there was an empty bottle. Well I was not surprised when she appeared; this woman who said she hits the pillow and never hears anything 'til morning! Well never mind. We sat in this threesome and it was not long before the conversation deteriorated and world war three started. This elderly woman was revealing what others in the family had said. Then out of the blue, "Janette, you have been married three times." I denied it of course, as what had it to do with here and now? There were lots of things I had done to keep my children together, and had worked hard and had lots of suffering and pain to go with it, but Phil just kept on repeating it. In the end he looked over at his Mother and said "She has hasn't she Mother?"

"Yes." Was her reply; how did she know this? I had never told anyone. It all came together; she had obviously been snooping round when I had left her on her own. Oh how dreadful these sad people are. "I have been married three times. I would have told you when the time was right. I can't see what difference it makes to our love and relationship at this time in our lives. After all the dreadful things your son and estranged wife have done to me; but you don't hear me complaining." With that he started shouting and swearing, calling me dreadful things and asking his old Mother for back up. I held my ground but was getting very upset. In the end his Mother intervened, "Stop now, Phil. Janette gave you your life back with all the love and attention. She gave you a reason to live and you are the first to say it. I should never have told you." Well she was right there. God knows what else they talk about, as I have heard them before talking about the other brother's children. With that there was a silence, "Janette I am so sorry; please forgive me. I should never have put you through that. You are so sweet; you don't deserve all this." With that he scooped me onto his knee and kissed me 'til it took my breath away. His mother sidled off to bed and Phil and I were once again on the planet which I would wish to stay. But it would not be for long, seeing as how these strange minded people viewed me as a threat as if I lead this loving life!

It was another day, and well, we needed our space and some air, so we decided to take a ride to Cleethorpes. We arrived and the weather was kind, so we decided to walk along the front, breathing in the sea air. Phil was very quiet, he must have been musing.

The next time he spoke, I found myself in the same position as on one very hot day in Albia, when we were walking my friend's dog, up the two miles to the lighthouse. He started to accuse me of something that had happened two years before I had met him. After long accusation, he realized and said "What the f--- is wrong with me? Why am I doing this to the only person who has truly showed me love in my life?" We had reached a beautiful part of the walk and were looking over a wall at the yachts bobbing about in the cove and people jumping into the sea. "I think I am going to buy a boat. Would you like that, Janette?" Before I could answer he continued, "Better still, let's just jump while we're happy and have each other, and that would be the end. Swimming forever, you and me with the dolphins."

"No Phil, what about poor Frankie the dog?" He burst into laughter "Just like you Janette, thinking of everyone. This is something I have come to know and love about you." After that we shared a kiss and were on our way as though nothing had been said.

So as we pursued our walk at Cleethorpes, I was being blamed for saying something I had never heard of, also at a time when I was not in Phil's life; I think his mind must have been searching for a reason to keep treating me so badly. A lot of it I could deal with because I have a lot of experience of bad behaviour from men in my life.

Jealousy works in so many guises and makes us hurt people we don't mean to. Still, we got through another day with lots of apologising from Phil once again.

Chapter Fifteen

The next day we were on our way home to York. It was good to be going back to my home with Phil; I knew he would be leaving me soon to go back to work, with all this confusion inside him still. I hoped to let us enjoy the drive home, but that wasn't going to last long. Driving along, Phil quietly spoke but I did not hear. "What did you say darling? I didn't quite catch what you said."

"I was just talking, it has fuck all to do with you." Well the monster had returned; I believe his mother had some lasting effect on him. "No wonder your Mother said you were a manic depressive and had to have a psychiatrist when you were young and on board the submarine. Your behaviour towards me is shocking."

"Is this the kind of thing my Mother is going round saying about me? Well what an absolute shit."

"Well let's just stop this right there and be two adults who have fallen in love and stop being influenced by smaller minded people."

"You're so right; I am so out of order, so sorry."

"Let's not be sorry, let's just be our own people." He grabbed my hand and gave it a squeeze "You're mine, all mine. I am so lucky. I know you will always be there for me. I love you so much."

"The same." was my response then we were happily on our way home again. It was heaven to be home, feeling relaxed and happy once again. "I don't want you to cook. I will take us out for a meal. You have done enough putting up with all this behaviour from me." Well I was all for going out, so we had a little relax then got ourselves ready. Phil wanted to go to the Indian as he had enjoyed it so much the last time, and I was happy to go along with whatever made him happy.

After a lovely meal, we started to walk home. We called at a quaint pub near my home; there was a quiz on and we joined in so it was a nice night! As we continued our walk home, things were so good and Phil kept stopping every hundred yards to tell me how much he wanted to spend his life with me and live in York and Spain with me. It was nice as I loved him so much but did worry about his erratic behaviour. Snuggled in my big bed, I felt so safe, as though there wasn't a care or another person in the world!

The next day my grandchildren came; Jack and Jill. I was so pleased to see them. They liked Phil so that was good. They had met him previously so it was easy. We decided to take the children out for a walk and some lunch; we took a nice leisurely walk along the river. We were all chatting and laughing and singing, so it made me happy as I love all my grandchildren so much. We reached *Plonkers*, where we ate. Phil decided to go and buy tickets for that evening from *The Grand Opera House* for a sixties revival band; so we had to hurry back home to prepare ourselves for the evening. We were a little worried the children wouldn't like it but they loved it. The bands were fantastic, so I felt so happy. But once again the devil took hold. Phil spoke to me but the music was so loud, "Sorry darling I didn't hear what you said."

"I was just fucking speaking to you." I totally ignored him; what was wrong with this man? Next everyone was standing up and dancing in the aisle, so I got up and got the grandchildren up. We were having such fun, and then Phil got up and was so happy. He squeezed my hand but this was all getting to be too much.

When we arrived home, everyone was feeling tired so it was straight to bed. When everyone was settled I went quietly up. I sidled into bed, then a voice said, "Are you annoyed with me?"

"Yes Phil, this time I am. You just seem so hell bent on spoiling every lovely thing we do."

"I am so sorry, you're right. I can't seem to stop. It's like something has been eating away at me all my life and you are the person I am able to vent it on as you have this special forgiveness."

"Well I have, but we must sort it out and put it in the right perspective, so we can go forward and have this lovely life we both deserve."

"I support that wholly and long for the time when I won't ever be out of order with you again. Goodnight darling, I don't deserve you. But I will show you I do; I am going to buy a ring!" I laid for a long time thinking of what he had said, then drifted off into a pleasant sleep.

The next day came so quickly; soon Phil was sat in the car, ready for going. In the house he had said his goodbyes and kissed me in front of the children, saying "I love your

Nana very much and will be back for her soon, take care of her for me. She is so precious." The little darlings went "Awww" (bless them!) Phil kept me calling to the car and kissing me.

"I don't want to go."

"Well don't!" But in the end he pulled away, shouting through the window "I love you!" He papped his horn and then he was gone. It felt so lonely, but I had my lovely grandchildren there so it didn't feel so bad.

Chapter Sixteen

All the rest of the day we busied ourselves. Jack went off to play football and we girls had a quiet night in. After my darlings went to bed, I stayed up watching a film while about 1 a.m. but no word came from Phil. Although I was missing him I soon found sleep. I was thinking "He has gone back into the hornets nest. What will happen next? I have no idea. With these people in his life who confuse his train of thought, he cannot see through the fog."

On Sunday night I was alone. I decided to call Phil's mum, hoping he hadn't gone but just wanting to know if he had got off okay. "Hello Janette, Phil was upset last night. He said he didn't want to leave you, and asked me to call you as he needed to speak with you."

"Well you can't have, seeing as it was about 11.30 p.m."

"I just said you must be out." Well this woman had rung my house numerous times, so she was once again keeping us apart (how evil!) "He was most upset as he had wanted to speak with you." So how could she do such a thing? Well he had the option to ring me; once again I am left in this state of suspense. I spoke to Phil briefly on the phone; he said he loved me and was sorry he had gone back to Spain too soon, or shouldn't have gone back at all. "I'm planning all my flights and area for work so I am busy. Now I am here I might as well go and earn some money for us; I will call you later. I am at Dennis' at the moment." Well that is another situation he would be best out of. I left him to it. Friday would bring another different story, but who can predict? If only.

Chapter Seventeen

On Friday the 4th of November people were staying at my house. In the evening we took them to the local to eat. The grandchildren had a lovely time as did my friend. We got the children down to sleep, then the grownups went; it had been a hectic night. I just sat downstairs quietly, but could not stop thinking there was something not right. I dialled '1471' and found a Spanish number had called; it was Phil's. I rang his number straight away, "Janette I knew you would call. I have not been drinking as I have been sat waiting for the boys to come – my sons. I wanted to talk with them and tell them as much as I could about what my intentions are with you and my future, but they have not come. Janette I feel so lost without you and it has been a long road. I must now treat you right as you deserve. I should never have come back without you; I left your home far too soon."

"I told you so, but I am always here to support you."

"Janette please be quiet and let me say what I have to say; then I can open my wine and have a drink. Janette I love you and I want you to marry me. I want full commitment from you and to know you're mine."

"Phil you have full commitment from me and I couldn't love you more than I do. We haven't got to that stage yet with your previous marriage."

"You have married other men; why not me?"

"I want to marry you more than anything, but you need to close the other one first."

The next thing he said put a fear in me that I had felt before, "If you don't marry me, I don't want to go on living. Everything I have thought out and planned for us would be pointless. Now can I open my bottle and have a drink?"

"Please, please Phil, don't put me in this position. I love you so much and you are so far away from me. I don't want the rest of my life without you in it; it has been such a hard journey up to here, but also a lovely one. I will stay on this phone for as long as it takes to get you to see reason and see a wonderful future together, as soon as you get back from this trip." I spoke to him for over three hours until he said he was feeling happy and tired, and he would call me and send a lovely email on the 5th. "God bless my darling and thank you for making me feel secure, safe and loved." I was exhausted. It was 3.30 a.m. so I crawled into bed and was gone. Thank goodness everyone slept 'til later. Still another day had dawned; what would it bring from Phil?

The day of the 5th of November was my grandson's birthday. We were all going out for the evening, so it was all hustle and bustle with not a lot of time for moping. I did check on my emails later in the afternoon but there was nothing from Phil. Also I tried to ring him a couple of times but it just went to answer machine. Did I deserve this – the stress, the worry? No. So I decided to try to put it to the back of my mind, for I did not want to spoil the party.

It was rather late when we got home. I checked everything but nothing from Phil. I didn't deserve this treatment after all I had gone through with him, yet again, the night before. I went to bed but could not sleep; I just cried and stressed and worried. I think I found sleep around 4.30 a.m. but was woken again around 6.30 a.m.

Sunday was unbelievable; just waiting, stressing, and calling a phone which was never answered. How cruel people could be; surely someone would let me know. I spent the night in my bed crying, saying "Why? Why? What evil has got inside him now?"

The next Monday, the 7th November, I had things to do. In the evening I sat and drank and chatted with a friend, "I am going to bed Janette; I am tired. You need to too if you're so poorly." I didn't know quite how so poorly I would be in the unforeseeable future.

In desperation I rang Phil's brother's house in Spain; it was late but I could stand no more. I did not want to have to speak to them, as I found they had become quite intolerable with their wicked weaving; but here I was talking to Damian, "Do you know what time it is?"

"Yes, I just want to know if Phil is with you."

"No he isn't."

"Well please, have you seen him?"

"Yes he's fine; we have all been out for a Chinese meal." My reaction was quiet justifiable, "You bastards you fucking bastards. You have made me suffer for yet another three days; how wicked you all are." I put the phone down and cried myself to sleep, feeling so let down once again. What kind of a person would do this to me?

On Wednesday the 9th November, as I expected there was a brief email from Phil, "I know I am wrong and should have been in touch with you; I'm very sorry. I am flying back to the rig today and I will put everything right. Love you." Well what did he think? With all the pain and the worry I have suffered once again these past few days, that a short email makes it okay? When only a few days previous, I was on the phone for over three hours when he was virtually torturing me with his emotional threats of not wanting to live if I didn't marry him. Then not being in contact. What was I dealing with? I sent him an email which did not much please him; I realised his behaviour, as before, was not only selfish, but cruel, unbalanced and damn right disgusting to a person who loved him with sincerity.

Chapter Eighteen

I believe the next part of my life and the year ahead has been the total cause of my illness – the stress and constant up and down has all but nearly ended my life, only my strength of living has made me go on.

His mother and I were still in contact, her telling me "Phil has rung you and told you it is over."

"I think I know who has called me, and not one was from Mr Harrison. Your son is a liar. He has never given me closure from this relationship; not that it is any business of yours." Then the next time, "He says he misses you and your kisses and cuddles." What kind of a man had I fallen for? Tittle-tattling to an elderly woman instead of speaking to the woman he should – me!!!

That Christmas and New Year was spent in Spain with my youngest son. We stayed at my friend's, looking after pets whilst she was in England. It was the lovely and warm, but my heart was yearning for an answer from the man I can only call a coward. But he did not appear.

I saw my friend Kyle; he came to where I was staying and had a drink with my son and myself. He spoke very badly about Phil; it seems he is not well thought of. But my son said, "Mum liked him, that's all that mattered. It's sad about his behaviour."

2012 became so sad for me – crying myself to sleep night after night, hoping he would call or email; but no, nothing. In the March I had my first stroke; all through the heartache I was suffering. I made a good recovery and got the use back in my legs within a few days, so I came out and stayed with my family. Soon it was another hospital trip; the man in charge said I would be able to go on a short flight, so I returned to my friend's at the end of May. They were now living in Albia. My two weeks went quickly, but one evening in the wonderful cocktail bar, we sensed a scene was about to erupt.

A tall, pretty, well-built blonde came to join our company with her man-friend. She seemed to know me, but not I her. She was drinking heavily and started talking about Phil in such an abusive manner; her language was something else, and her – a business woman! Gunter started, "Phil's wife works in my office; I lived with one of their sons for sometime and I can only tell you he is a shit. A fucking t**t, a no good fucking rat." So it went on,

"I don't wish to know and can live without your foul mouth about someone I love. I can take care of my own affairs." Well she never stopped, but did calm down, so the rest of our evening was spent pleasantly getting wrecked.

We got a taxi back to my friend's, and sitting out on the warm balcony so high up, I wondered what I had done to deserve all this. After just two people falling in love at such a mature age and Phil being alone for so long, what kind of threat was I?

It was the beginning of June when I returned. My heart was all over the place and I did not feel well. Phil's Mum rang and I told her about the woman. "I've never heard of her."

"Well she has been in the family ten years and part of the family work in her office."

"Oh it will be some woman who Phil has given the push back." Well I couldn't stop laughing and had to get off the phone. I think my body and soul was on overdrive and on July 1st I had another stroke. This time it took the sight in my right eye and right peripheral. Two weeks later another stroke blocked my left.

My health was now so unbelievable, I had lost my sight. Sight is such a precious gift to people who are lucky enough to have it. I have always loved life and kept on smiling no matter what. I am still smiling and I do not look any different, but looking from my side it is a totally different story.

The next few weeks were spent trying to come to terms with this. I stayed with my family. Phil's Mother knew what had happened but still there was no call from him. Well would you expect it? I have come to the conclusion that he is a coward about life and cannot give closure as you don't get any medicine for it (answers.)

The next few months involved lots of hospital visits; getting myself on different treatments, well looked after by consultants, registrars, staff of all aspects, and I am now known as the ambassador of strokes – well a new title!

I had my darling granddaughter take me off various things on my laptop, as I was finding it hard to deal with

Facebook etc. I just needed it to do my many stories and poems I have written. I kept in touch briefly on the phone with Phil's Mum, but found it difficult.

It was the start of November 2012. On Sunday I was calling my friend's English number as she was visiting England from Spain, but unfortunately I rang the wrong number. A male answered, "Hello?" I thought is was a familiar voice, "Is that Janette?" then followed a laugh, well more of a little giggle, "Who am I speaking to?" Silence reigned but they did not put the phone down; I did. I called back the same number after finishing what I was doing, but of course as I knew it was now on answering machine. Phil had always, always said "As soon as I hear your voice, the need to be near you is overwhelming." So nothing had changed.

In the meantime, things went along in the wondering stage. It was almost two weeks before I had Phil's Mum on the phone. Our conversation was just normal, asking each other what we had been doing. "Oh I rang Phil's number by mistake the other week."

"Well I didn't know anything about that"

"Well why should you?"

"Because I see him a lot."

"Oh are you flying to Spain every couple of weeks?"

"No, he is living here now and has gone back on the rig. It's a disgrace, that Leanne – after money all the time, and her working under a false name in her son's office in Spain."

"Well let me just say when did he go back on the rig?"

"This Thursday."

"Well can I just remind you, it was a couple of weeks

ago I said I had rang his number, so I don't need you telling me who and when I rang. Also it is my business if I want to write a book." With that she started a vicious attack on me, "Well he isn't with me anymore; he's in a house with a woman. I didn't want to tell you." I thought, "Not much." She continued,

"He never wanted to spend his life with you; you were just available at the time." This was the old lady I had taken under my wing, who now turns out to be an evil, old, bitter, jealous woman. No wonder Phil is like he is with such a dysfunctional family. "I do not wish to speak to you any further. Goodbye."

I looked at my laptop to see if my Facebook account had been cancelled, as I had asked my granddaughter a couple of months earlier to take me off, as my sight problem was making it all so difficult. We found about twenty five failed messages from postmaster; at least fifteen of them were from Mr Phil Higgins, from September, October and November 2012. We opened a couple; one said "Phil Higgins likes your new picture", the next one said "When I was young I asked God for a bike, but God doesn't work like that, so I stole one. But he forgave me. How about you? Will you forgive me?" I could not bear to look at anymore, as my pain had never gone. Why hadn't he taken the easy route, seeing as he was now just over an hour away from me, to talk, to ring, but his emails contradicted everything that woman had said to me. Also she was in our very hearts and souls; what a destructive being, and to think she knew the very things she said would give me such total stress. That has been the whole essence of my illness, through PHIL HIGGINS behaviour towards our love, madness, hurt and emotional blackmail. This has never had closure, so the wound stays open and just gets deeper.